ATOMIC
KITCHEN

GADGETS AND INVENTIONS FOR YESTERDAY'S COOK

BRIAN S. ALEXANDER

PORTLAND, OREGON

Book Design: Vicki Knapton and Wade Daughtry
Project Manager: Jennifer Weaver-Neist
Editors: Ann Granning Bennett and Summer Steele

Library of Congress Cataloging-in-Publication Data

Alexander, Brian S.
  Atomic kitchen : gadgets and inventions for yesterday's cook / Brian Alexander.— 1st American ed.
      p. cm.
  ISBN 1-888054-98-0 (pbk. : alk. paper)
  1. Kitchen utensils — History — 20th century. I. Title.
   TX656.A44 2004
   683'.82'0904--dc22
                              2004015595

Printed in Singapore

9 8 7 6 5 4 3 2 1

Collectors Press books are available at special discounts for bulk purchases, premiums, and promotions. Special editions, including personalized inserts or covers, and corporate logos, can be printed in quantity for special purposes. For further information contact: Special Sales, Collectors Press, Inc., P.O. Box 230986 Portland, OR 97281. Toll free: 1-800-423-1848.

For a free catalog write: Collectors Press, Inc., P.O. Box 230986, Portland, OR 97281. Toll free: 1-800-423-1848 or visit our website at: collectorspress.com.

CONTENTS

INTRODUCTION

In one sense the term "atomic kitchen" is a fun way of describing a streamlined, labor-saving, 1950s super kitchen, offering the ultimate in Space Age modern convenience, ease, and beauty. But it's also a term appropriate for its time — one that illustrates the optimism that housewives held for the future.

If the concept of using atomic power for kitchen appliances seems almost unbelievable today, it must not have appeared so in the 1950s. A typical housewife probably would have accepted it as a definite possibility, likely to be realized by the year 2000, because the 1950s was a period of boundless optimism, with a "reach-for-the-stars" mentality.

Let's look at some of the factors that helped bring about this optimism. The end of World War II and the immediate postwar period set the stage for much of what was to come. The drawn-out anticipation of when the war would be over, families reunited, and life back to normal, in combination with rationing of many consumer goods, led to a continual postponement of a better life to come. Thus, a sort of dream mentality took hold, focusing largely on when desired products would be available. (A good example of this is the lengthy build-up before the introduction of

television.) Everyone seemed to be planning for a future of wonderful things. Manufacturers were more than eager to play off these hopes by offering long-desired "dream" products for the American marketplace.

Foremost among these were products for the kitchen of the future lingering in the minds of many housewives. The following is an excerpt from a 1948 Youngstown Kitchen brochure:

> "Presto . . . that dream kitchen comes true . . . Just as you've always imagined it . . . right down to the last square inch of shelf and storage space! Not a chance to waste a step . . . not a pot or pan out of place! . . . and what a work-saving beauty it is! Morning, noon or night . . . you sail through kitchen routines hardly realizing you're doing kitchen chores. That's how much a Youngstown Kitchen lightens your work! . . . Oh what magic! From the time you fill that morning coffee pot, your kitchen helps you perform every task. Seeing that youngsters have a good, hot breakfast . . . fixing lunches . . . stacking dishes, washing, rinsing, and putting them away . . . Lady, your kitchen will work magic. Look at the kitchens on this page . . . kitchens with a bright future for you!"

A number of manufacturers advertised their products as the best and most innovative, proudly proclaiming their models "the first totally new postwar designs." This boasting by companies led to even more expectations on the part of consumers and to a continual cycle of innovation. The most common example of this was the annual model change of automobiles from Detroit, even if the actual "change" was little more than a face-lift. This is evident when comparing autos from 1948 to 1958 with those of the prior decade, when styling wasn't as much an issue.

The family kitchen, long overdue for improvement, finally started to receive added attention from manufacturers and suppliers in the late 1940s and 1950s. Here was

the heart of the home, much as the hearth had been in earlier times. No longer merely the meal preparation center, it was now a meeting place for daily activities. Any enterprising businessman on his way up would want to upgrade this area for the benefit of the lady of the house, making her life easier and transforming the outlook of the entire family.

Leading the way in this effort was the development of new and improved electrical appliances. For many years, kitchen appliances, such as toasters and mixers, were somewhat awkward-looking and not especially attractive. They were intended to be stored in a cupboard and out of sight after use. In the 1930s and 1940s manufacturers determined that by adding a few stylistic touches such as bright trim and streamlined contours, their products were more likely to be left on the counter or table, increasing visibility and use. As companies addressed the issue of making their products better, the trend to improve appearance continued with added emphasis. Immediately after the war most appliances were still in demand regardless of style. However in the 1950s, style and color selection became of increasing importance for companies wanting their products to be perceived as desirable.

Although kitchenware in color wasn't a new concept — colorful objects for kitchen use began appearing in the 1920s — its increased availability and emphasis was. Color took center stage with the introduction of color television in 1954, and now that the future was set to be a more colorful one, most companies wanted to get on the bandwagon. This trend to color wasn't limited to a few accent pieces. In many instances, 1950s décor meant wall-to-wall saturation where even the smallest color detail might be

included. Styling and color options helped many manufacturers stand out from the crowd, but in some instances this meant emphasizing color in lieu of any real product improvement. A primary example of this is the Sunbeam color-coordinated frying pan introduced in the mid 1950s. Although having a choice of yellow, turquoise, or pink for a frying pan could be seen as a new option, it did little to mask the fact that the product was essentially the same as before.

As many of the most popular electrical appliances came into wide acceptance in the 1950s, companies began introducing new products and improvements to increase sales, leading to an overall increase in the number of products in use. One study determined that the typical kitchen in the late 1930s had about five electrical appliances, whereas twenty years later that number had increased to twelve or more. Manufacturers were more than eager to show how "heat-controlled" frying pans, and larger capacity toasters and waffle bakers made older versions seem obsolete. Deluxe coffee makers, blenders, and knife sharpeners all became necessities for a well-equipped kitchen. Forward-looking homemakers were now likely to have an electric can opener, countertop rotisserie oven, and specialty devices for popping corn, baking beans, and crushing ice.

Once all these electrical marvels were in use, secondary needs came to the fore-front for the 1950s housewife. Wouldn't it be better if your appliances had an inter-changeable power element for convenience, ease of cleaning, and economy? Introduced by Presto in the mid 1950s, this concept spread like wildfire through the small-appliance field. And with this bevy of electrical helpers at hand, what should you do about all those power cords at your outlet? Described in a period article as the "small appliance bugaboo," you had to overcome this if you wanted to avoid "bedlam" in your kitchen. One solution was a stylish, integrated appliance center built right into your cabinets. Easily within reach, it offered multiple outlets

for your appliances and an integral timer as well. The more adventurous could install a Nutone built-in food center. It offered a variety of appliances for use with one motor, conveniently embedded in your countertop. According to one of their ads it was "the last word for a modern kitchen!"

With all the emphasis on style and product improvement, it's easy to overlook another compelling factor influencing families and housewives of the 1950s. Viewing a few vintage television commercials makes this immediately clear. It's the impression your shiny new purchase would make on family, friends, or neighbors. Together with new cars, appliances, and other major purchases, this status of ownership became an important factor. A line from a 1950s car commercial went, "There's Mr. Williams driving by in his new Star Cruiser, just look at the admiring glances he gets from his neighbor Mr. Smith." For the typical housewife, the stodgy old stoves and refrigerators of a few years earlier just couldn't compete with the color and chrome of a new model festooned with the latest features and doodads.

In the 1950s those planning to host a party could select from a wide range of fun serving pieces and gadgets to make work easier and amuse guests. Why serve with ordinary dishes when you could use a novel fold-out serving buffet? When piled high with goodies, it was certain to get attention. Aluminum glasses and accessories in a rainbow of colors would help set a bright note, while stream-lined designs for ice crushers and buckets looked like they could survive a space voyage and enliven any party setting.

Companies with products not usually thought of as innovative tried for additional appeal by stressing novel designs and uses. Thus, for small kitchens, you might want to install pullman-style cabinets where the bottom half folds down to create

The 1933 Chicago Century of Progress Exposition featured an unique glimpse of the future with its House of Tomorrow.

WALL
REFRIGERATOR-
FREEZER

New G-E Wall Refrigerator comes in these Mix-or-Match colors: Canary Yellow, Turquoise Green, Petal Pink, Cadet Blue, Woodtone Brown—or White.

So much room for all your foods

1. 11 cubic feet of space. 2. Big automatic-defrost refrigerator section. 3. Permanent General Electric Alnico Magnetic Doors provide sure seal . . . close silently. 4. Separate vegetable and fruit compartments. 5. Adjustable door shelves for small jars and cans. 6. 2-cubic-foot true zero-degree food freezer holds up to 70 pounds or 83 packages. 7. New-style Mini-Cube® ice trays. 8. Dependable and whisper-quiet sealed-in General Electric refrigeration system. 9. Complete unit is 64 inches long, 39½ inches high, 17⅞ inches deep.

Progress Is Our Most Important Product

GENERAL 🄶🄴 ELECTRIC

AFTER

BEFORE

19

How to be very, very Happy in a Kitchen

a countertop, and the top part folds up to reveal shelves. When closed, these cabinets gave your kitchen a novel, sleek look and kept practically every object out of sight. Can't decide between wood or metal cabinets? Just install one company's reversible cabinet fronts, and you can have the advantages of both. One scheme even illustrated a floor that could do more. Just pull up a few pillows and snacks and play a game of checkers or chess on a game board inlaid with tile right on your kitchen floor, but, we hope, not in the way of someone raiding the icebox.

By the late 1950s, new and exciting themes of atomic energy and space travel emerged to keep product designs fresh for consumers. This Space Age mentality helped inspire designers whose imagination was fueled by images of Superman or the Jetsons soaring through the sky on television. Its influence can't be denied as rocket, atomic, or amoeba shaped patterns spread across the landscape, even if it did spawn such exaggerated motifs as tailfins on cars and push-button gimmickry.

Although Russia beat the U.S. into space with Sputnik, marketers made sure we would be first with Space Age improvements for the kitchen. Here the boundaries of your ceiling and windows could be pushed upward, revealing huge expanses of light and space. A myriad of built-in appliances would help insure an up-to-date, modern look. Color could now enhance every component of your work space. Having a matched stove and refrigerator without using the same color on your washer and dryer was almost heresy. However even the most atomic of kitchens from the late 1950s would usually have an antique pot or accessory on display. Because, then as now, even the most futuristic kitchen can seem cold and sterile if it doesn't connect somehow with the past.

THE EVOLUTION OF THE ATOMIC KITCHEN

1

Since the earliest times, kitchen designs have continued to evolve. Since the age where cooking activities centered around a fireplace with primitive iron utensils, there has been an ongoing effort to improve the utility and appearance of this important area of the home.

An early influence on kitchen designs and homemakers was Catherine Beecher in the nineteenth century. Her 1869 book, *The American Woman's Home,* co-authored with her more famous sister Harriet Beecher Stowe, included plans and illustrations for an efficient kitchen along with other domestic topics. She showed how grouping similar activities together, such as food preparation, baking, and cleaning, could make tasks easier and more economical. Beecher's work was highly popular at the time and went through several printings. It continued to be an influence in later kitchen design and planning.

Starting in the late nineteenth century, new publications, such as *The Ladies Home Journal,* took up the cause for domestic issues and helped set standards for homemakers. Readers were curious about the lifestyles of others and welcomed information about the latest products for kitchen and home. Although few readers could keep up with the rapid pace of development of the early twentieth century, periodicals were important in helping consumers visualize what their home or kitchen potentially could look like.

By the 1930s this interest in seeing what might be in the future had evolved into "Kitchens of Tomorrow" displays staged by manufacturers. Here companies used elaborate demonstration kitchens to showcase their newest developments in product design and planning. These typically featured all-electric appliances, accessories, and built-in sinks and cabinets with streamlined styling. They became successful marketing tools for companies, such as General Electric, Westinghouse, and Roper Stoves, and helped speed the introduction of dishwashers, sink disposals,

kitchen telephones, and other products. Demonstration kitchens were sure to draw the attention of any homemaker still using "Hoosier" Cabinets* or ice boxes from earlier decades. (This disparity between old versus new was humorously shown in the 1948 movie *The Further Adventures of Ma and Pa Kettle,* when Pa wins an ultra-modern dream home.)

Showcasing advanced designs and products took a step forward at the Chicago Century of Progress Exposition in 1933, where thirteen model homes were built to display the latest innovations. These homes included a variety of styles and new construction materials such as modular steel, artificial stone, and the glass and steel "House of Tomorrow."

The House of Tomorrow (see page 18) with its twelve-sided shape, central support core, and first-floor airplane hangar was a magnet for fair goers. Visitors marveled at its air conditioning, Art Deco furnishings, and the streamlined Pierce Silver Arrow show car parked outside, making it a runaway hit at the fair. The sleek kitchen included stainless steel counters and sinks and a wall of built-in metal cabinets. The latest in electrical appliances and accessories were shown, including a built-in dishwasher and exhaust fan. This house is still a home with a future today, as it and other display homes were barged across Lake Michigan after the fair to help promote the new resort town of Beverly Shores, Indiana. Today these homes continue to maintain their lakefront presence as part of the Indiana Dunes National Lakeshore.

The 1939 New York World's Fair also included an enclave of model homes called the "Town of Tomorrow," which was somewhat larger and more traditionally oriented than the homes at Chicago's fair. Again, the latest new products for the home and ideas in kitchen planning were shown to fair visitors and a new curiosity made its appearance, television. The modern-home model included a streamlined all-electric

*The Hoosier Cabinet of the early 1900s revolutionized the kitchen. Standing in one place, the homemaker could sift flour, measure ingredients, mix dough, and roll it out on a porcelain ledge. It contained a flour bin, carousel spice racks, cooking charts, spice grinder, and more.

GE kitchen and attracted a continuous stream of visitors. A full assortment of small appliances were on display including a Triple-Whip mixer, coffee maker, automatic toaster, waffle baker, and kitchen clock and timer. The built-in ventilation fan boasted it could renew the air in the kitchen every two to three minutes.

Forward-looking homes in the 1940s would draw upon ideas already proposed to help alleviate the postwar housing shortage. These included the Lustron Home, with modular steel construction already seen at the 1933 Chicago Exposition. It was a five-room, modern ranch home with exterior and interior walls and roof made from porcelain-enameled steel. More compact and efficient than earlier modular homes, the Lustron Home took the process a step further by establishing an extensive dealer network. Every detail of the Lustron Home was planned for efficiency and ease of use. A few special features were added for housewives to make the home seem even more modern and desirable. Easy-to-clean steel shelving in the kitchen included an integral pass-through to the dining room, and a built-in dishwasher next to the sink. These and other built-ins, such as a china cabinet and master bedroom vanity, helped win over many potential buyers. Although there were high initial expectations for the Lustron Home and the company was able to secure substantial government loans, it never lasted far beyond the postwar period. Between 1947 and 1950, about 2,500 of the homes were built around the country.

As steel modular homes went from concept to reality in the 1950s, visionary thinkers forecasting future trends for housing turned to an obvious material for inspiration, plastics. In 1953 Monsanto, a major plastics company, sponsored a research project with MIT to develop an all-plastic house. After the initial concept was developed, a demonstration plastic home, the Monsanto "House of the Future," was erected at Disneyland and opened for visitors in 1957 (see pages 50 and 51). The home was built with four cantilevered plastic bays radiating from a small central core and foundation. The basic plan was comprised of sixteen large

plastic sections, but could be enlarged by adding additional units. Plastics were used extensively throughout the home, but other materials, such as concrete, steel, and wood, were used where advantageous.

The kitchen in the Monsanto House included several of the latest appliances and a number of innovative concepts as well. It was equipped with a shelf-height refrigerator, microwave oven, and a wall communication center with a television and push-button telephone. A futuristic innovation was the ultrasonic dishwasher and storage compartment, with a top that folded down to serve as a planning and work desk. Some of the features shown, such as plastic foam upholstery and a Tupperware glass carrier, were quickly adopted by consumers, while others, like a height-adjustable lavatory for youngsters, still would be a novelty today. Even after a total refurbishing in the 1960s, the Monsanto House had difficulty keeping up with the times and was dismantled in 1967. Today it is still fondly remembered by many who visited Disneyland.

About the same time Monsanto was erecting the House of the Future, RCA's Whirlpool appliance division built a traveling demonstration — "Miracle Kitchen" — that visited a number of U.S. cities in 1957. In addition to a few new products available at the time, such as a microwave oven and combination washer and dryer, the Miracle Kitchen included many features that would still be futuristic today. Many kitchen activities were remote-controlled from a central planning center, somewhat akin to today's computer. Here you could plan menus, monitor food supplies and check in on the nursery, or monitor guests at the door via closed-circuit TV. It also included several automatic food preparation devices and a hot-and-cold beverage dispenser that would fit right in with the world of George Jetson. A mobile floor sweeper that automatically cleaned your floor and mobile dishwasher and storage unit were also developments helpful for the busy mom of the future. According to a period brochure, with the Miracle Kitchen housewives were "at last entirely free of all the dull monotony of routine kitchen keeping."

Whirlpool's Miracle Kitchen comes closest to realizing the ideal of an atomic kitchen in the 1950s. Recent developments, such as robotic, computer-controlled sweepers and home monitoring devices, have made some of these advanced concepts a reality today.

Although kitchen planners of the past sometimes hit the mark with predictions for the future, they were less accurate in predicting the many processed and prepared foods available today that eliminate the need for many kitchen tasks or make them passé. While the future may relegate kitchen activities to reduced areas of space and attention, the heart-warming nature of kitchen experiences, the sights, smells, and sense of accomplishment they provide should remain a part of any future kitchen.

In other words, that favorite pie or other recipe shouldn't be put out to pasture just yet.

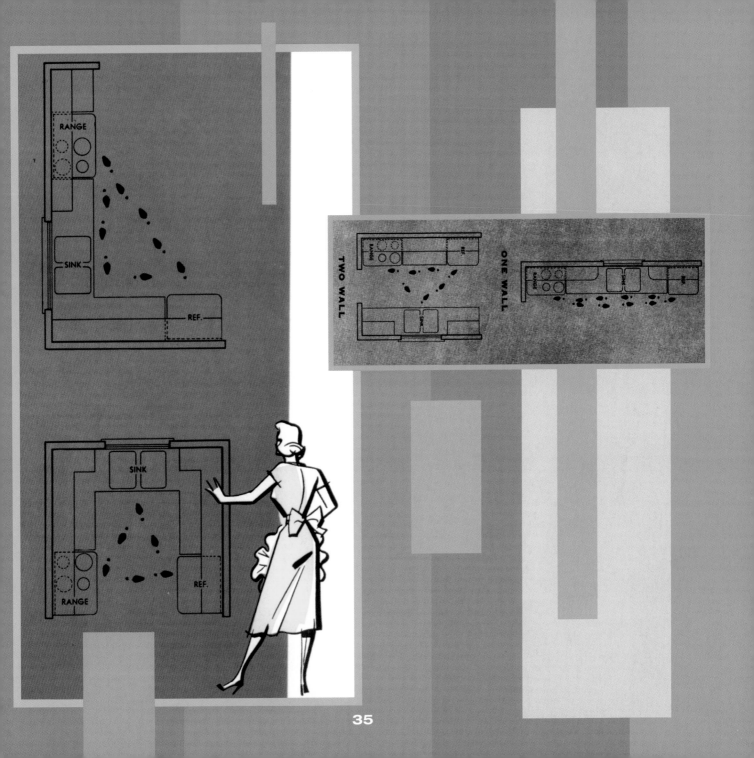

RANGE

SINK

REF.

SINK

RANGE

REF.

TWO WALL

ONE WALL

RANGE

REF.

SINK

RANGE

REF.

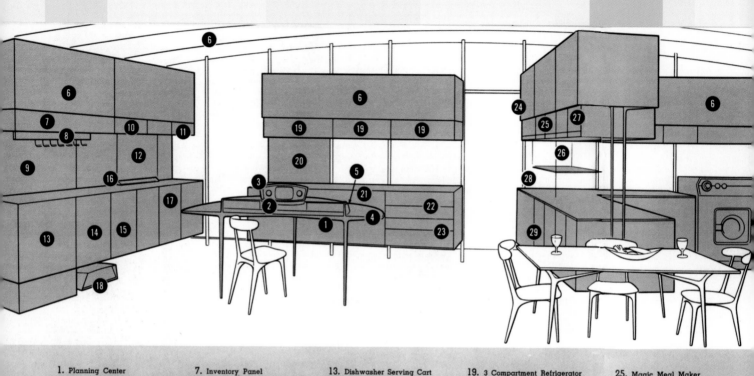

1. Planning Center
2. Remote Controls
3. TV Monitor
4. Cooking & Eating Surface
5. Electronic Air Purifying System
6. Mood Lighting Panels
7. Inventory Panel
8. Beverage Dispensers
9. Bottle Cooler
10. Package Food Storage
11. Mixing & Blending Unit
12. Recipe Viewer
13. Dishwasher Serving Cart
14. China Storage Compartment
15. Vegetable Storage Drawer
16. Custom Adjusted Sink
17. Vegetable Preparation Unit
18. Automatic Floor Cleaner
19. 3 Compartment Refrigerator
20. Mural Wall Television
21. Custom Sink
22. Salad Freshener
23. Freezer
24. Prepared Meals Storage
25. Magic Meal Maker
26. Electronic Oven
27. Electronic Cooking Unit
28. Mobile Cooking Unit
29. Utensil Storage Drawer
30. Washer-Dryer Combination

When General Electric unveiled their Kitchen of Tomorrow at the 1939 World's Fair in New York, one appliance was promoted with this jingle: "With a dish-washer so very fast and sanitary / She'd never break another dish 'twas plain / And the work she most despised / Was completely modernized / When the garbage went like magic down the drain."

After the huge participation of women in war-related jobs in the 1940s, women comprised about one-third of the workforce in the 1950s. Most held clerical jobs rather than production jobs.

Kromex gives your kitchen the
MODERN LOOK
you're dreaming of!
NO KITCHEN LOOKS REALLY MODERN WITHOUT Kromex
A smart start to the kitchen you've been waiting for—that's KROMEX WARE.
Modern gleaming aluminum—dreamline* design that glorifies utensils . . . lifts them right out of the pots-and-pans class. Even the handles and knobs of forever-cool bake-lite have a new modern look, a new hand-customed grip.
Modern cooking—more delicious, nutritious results because KROMEX covers fit snugly, you cook with less water, enjoy more flavorful foods, retain vitamins.
See KROMEX at your favorite store . . . you'll want the complete set to give your kitchen the modern look you get only with KROMEX.
Wherever Housewares Are Sold
*Copyrighted by Kromex Corporation 1947
Kromex
ENDURINGLY BEAUTIFUL
For the Modern Look in Your Kitchen
Cleveland 8, Ohio
Designed by DON MORTRUDE

THE ⓇCA *Whirlpool* MIRACLE KITCHEN

From 1947 to 1951 William Levitt boasted nearly 17,500 homes which were built on 6000 acres of potato fields east of Manhattan. Levittown, as it came to be known, helped relieve the postwar housing shortage and employed an army of workers, each specializing in one of 27 tasks.

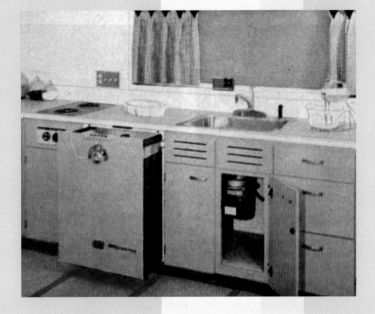

"My time's my Own . . . my kitchen is Kelvinator!"

Modern convenieces gave Mom more time for other endeavors. In 1961 Mary Kay Ash purchased a skin cream formula from the estate of a cosmetologist to form the nucleus of Mary Kay Cosmetics. The pink cadillac incentive program for sales leaders followed a few years later.

"SUBURBAN" DESIGN

HERE you see what is known as the U-shape kitchen design with the sink centered beneath this pretty picture window. This type of plan offers the utmost in convenience and easy operation at work centers. You'll have practically no cross-kitchen-traffic to hinder your easy steps from refrigerator to spacious sink, to the modern automatic cooking center. Note the corner wall cabinet with its full-view glass panel. It shows your favorite china and glassware to best advantage.

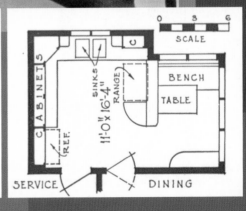

Swanson introduced the TV dinner in 1954 to satisfy the new eating habits of a TV-viewing public who had rearranged their furniture and lives to accommodate their favorite programs. Although the basic fare of a TV dinner paled in comparison to a home cooked meal, its convenience was a futuristic novelty.

For the Lady with a lot of living to do...

AMAZING NEW SPACE-MATES take only 25" of floor space . . . also install side by side. Laundromat, below, washes better, rinses better, cleans itself! Direct Air Flow Dryer fluffs and freshens clothes. Wash an 8 lb. load . . . dry an 8 lb. load at once.

DISPOSER
DISHWASHER
COOKING PLATFORMS
REFRIGERATOR & FREEZER
AUTOMATIC APPLIANCE CENTER
OVEN

SPACE-MATES

TRANSLUCENT WALL SCREEN

Modernist designer Russel Wright created a ceramic clock in a variety of earth tones for General Electric in 1952. It was designed to match the popular Russel Wright dinnerware available at the time.

People in the late 1950s and early 1960s were bombarded with information about the promise of science. According to *Science Digest*, atom powered wristwatches were just around the corner and nuclear powered autos were already being studied. It's no wonder that many housewives felt that atomic power would revolutionize their kitchens in the future.

The Hoover Constellation carpet sweeper from 1955 had a planet-shaped canister that "glided after you under its own power." It was an ideal compliment to modern Space Age décor.

Disneyland's Monsanto "House of the Future" was opened in 1957 and dismantled 10 years later.

The Cory Corp. introduced the Crown Jewel coffeemaker in 1954. Designed by Robert Budlong and trimmed in 24 carat gold with a melamine plastic handle, it sold for $50 and was successful with upscale shoppers.

Bring flower-fresh color to your table!

WEST BEND

Flavo-matic

THE AUTOMATIC PERCOLATOR

Illustrated above
DELPHINIUM BLUE

The West Bend Flavo-matic teams its talents with the loveliest flowers to create your most beautiful table setting. Cheery color . . . graceful design. And, it's nearly magic the way it *automatically* brews the best tasting coffee ever! Plug it in, starts to perk in seconds, shuts itself off when the coffee is ready, and keeps it at serving temperature. Makes 6 to 8 cups. Choice of three easy-to-clean colors . . . Delphinium Blue, Sunset Gold, Cherry Red. At housewares and appliance stores in the U. S. and Canada . . . $13.95*. (Also in polished aluminum, $11.95*)

Prices include excise tax.

SUNSET GOLD

CHERRY RED

WEST BEND ELECTRIC OVENETTE
Bakes and roasts like a regular oven...and saves 2/3 the electricity. 14-piece Ovenette includes roasting pan, pie pan, muffin...

WEST BEND ELECTRIC BEAN POT
Simmer-bakes beans to their flavorful best...with no effort! Genuine ceramic stoneware... 2 qt. size. Perfect, too, for stews, chili, soups...$6.95*

SUNSET GOLD

CHERRY RED

One of the first electric kettles was made in England and demonstrated in Chicago around the turn of the 20th Century. Not for the impatient, it took 12 minutes to boil a pint of water.

53

DORMEYER
Spring Carnival of Values!

Fri-Way Electric Skillet. New, immersible electric skillet has every convenience. All controls are on handle where they're easiest to use; big family-size frying area. Separate high dome copper-tone cover only $2.00.
Model 9301 **$19⁹⁵**

Big 4 to 10-Cup Coffee-Well. Chrome-finished aluminum coffee maker with no-drip spout and Dormeyer's famous dual heating controls. One control makes coffee to any strength, the other heats cold coffee without re-brewing. Has extra-wide opening for easy washing.
Model 6901 **$19⁹⁵**

Chrome Silver-Chef. Most impressive mixer you can own because it's of sparkling, never-stain chrome! Head is portable, has 10 different speeds, automatic beater release. Comes with 2 stainless steel bowls, exclusive $15.00 food grinder and pestle at no extra cost.
Model 4300 **$57⁵⁰**

New 9-Speed Portable Dormey. Here's the first 9-speed portable mixer in the world! Does every kind of mixing job yet is so lightweight it's not tiring to hold. Has full-size beaters, automatic beater release. In white, pink, turquoise, or yellow.
Model 9500 **$19⁹⁵**

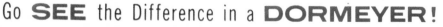

Go **SEE** the Difference in a **DORMEYER!**

This 6-piece economy set only $19.95

Regularly $23.20

The six most popular, most wanted Club pieces, to give "Full Flavor" goodness to meat, vegetables, poultry, fruit—and save time, work and fuel. Set includes:

1½-qt. Covered Saucepan (Cover fits 6¼" Fry Pan)	$3.45
2-qt. Covered Saucepan	$3.95
3-qt. Covered Saucepan	$4.45
4½-qt. Dutch Oven	$6.45
(Cover fits 10" Fry Pan to make Chicken Fryer)	
10-inch Fry Pan	$2.95
6¼-inch Fry Pan	$1.95
Regular price if purchased separately	$23.20

The cast aluminum Cook-and-Serve ware, designed by Dave Chapman for Club Aluminum in 1947, had an elegant, simulated, hammered finish. This popular design softened the mechanical look of aluminum, hid flaws, and was reminiscent of hand-worked antique silver.

Gifts for Better Living!

Oster Juicer-Slicer-Shredder

This wonderful new attachment gives the Osterizer extra food processing magic and added utility. Juices many different fruits and vegetables amazingly fast ... gives clear, fresh, delightfully tasty juices. It slices and shreds vegetables, fruits, coconut, cheese, etc. quickly and efficiently. Easy to clean.

Oster **Portable Electric Twins** **Meat Grinder**

The first electric meat grinder designed for home use. Compact. Powerful. Grinds all types of foods from toughest raw meats to hardest nut meats. Does more than the old hand grinder with none of the old struggle.

And the practical accessory gift

Oster Electric Ice Crusher HEAD

Fits on Meat Grinder Power Unit. It's quick and easy to attach and provides crushed ice of nine different size chips for every food or drink requirement.

DOUBLE ACTION Oster

Knife and Scissors Sharpener
Exclusive overlapping sharpening wheels hollow-grind both sides of blade at once. Sharpens scissors, too.

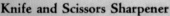

Oster KNEE ACTION

Portable Electric Mixer
The only food mixer that automatically adjusts to bowl contours. Three speeds. Finger-tip control. *Chrome, copper, white, and pastels.*

In 1964 the Ronson Corp. introduced the Can Do, a hand-held combination can opener, food mixer, and whipper. It also came with its own wall rack.

Rubbermaid Appliance Mat provides extra work space, protects appliance surface ... resists sliding. $2.98.

Rubbermaid Stove Mat keeps range work surface new-looking longer. Oven heat or hot pans can't damage. $2.49.

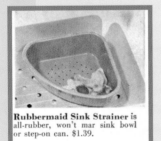

Rubbermaid Sink Strainer is all-rubber, won't mar sink bowl or step-on can. $1.39.

In a 1958 episode of *Alfred Hitchcock Presents* an acerbic and somewhat exasperated husband tells his wife, who is busily working in her fully applianced kitchen, "You don't prepare breakfast . . . you launch it like a missile."

he FRESH look!

In 1938 Formica, a durable, economical material for use on kitchen countertops, was first manufactured. Its use helped increase kitchen counter space, as it was less expensive than tile, porcelain enameled steel, stainless steel, and other materials in use at the time.

"I'm no longer tied to my kitchen apron strings!"

"Now *one* shopping trip does for weeks!"

"I can whip up a company dinner in half-an-hour!"

The first Joy Detergent bottle was designed by Deskey & Assoc. in 1950. It had a non-slip ribbed surface and was packaged in a carton to give the impression of greater size. The name "Joy" was chosen to help lessen the caustic drudgery usually associated with cleaning products.

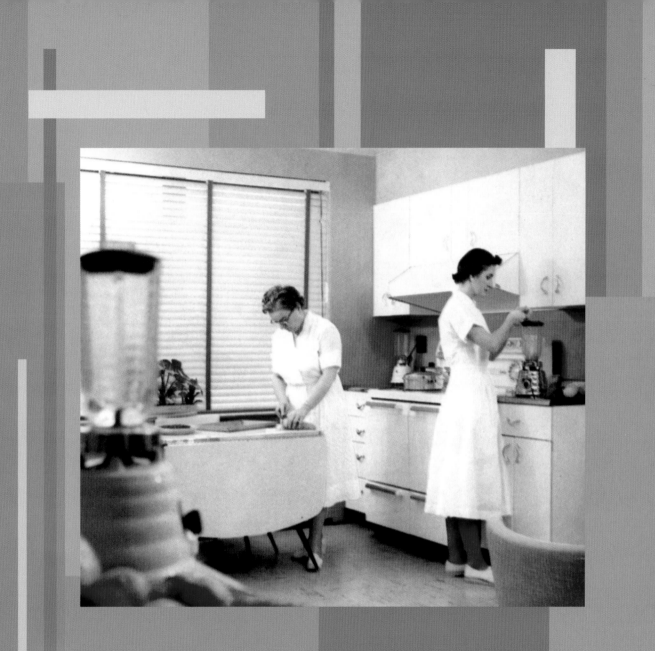

Dream Features and Cookware

2

In the early 1950s, the kitchen benefited greatly from advances in industrial technology and design, coupled with the optimistic outlook of homemakers. "Never before" was a catch phrase advertisers used to convey that a product was truly new and those buying it were living in a special time full of remarkable developments. When atomic energy was tapped to provide electricity in the mid 1950s, GE was on the scene to photograph the first hamburgers cooked with this new source of power. Consumers were advised that the kitchens of America were sure to be next in line to benefit from all the Atomic Age had to offer.

Manufacturers who wanted their products to stand out developed new features and designs to attract customers and motivate them to replace older models. In 1950 General Electric offered a Triple-Whip Mixer with three powerful beaters and a built-in light. This hybrid mixer design never caught on with consumers. GE did score a hit, however, with its Monotop counter surface in 1952. Once buyers got a look at an easy-to-clean, one-piece countertop, it made the standard stainless steel trim and separate backsplash models seem old-fashioned. In the late 1950s GE brought out a stylish flip-top Rotisserie Oven. Presented as a "second" oven, it offered infra-red broiling, automatic timer, and a rotisserie. The only question for most buyers was where to store it.

Refrigerator and stove manufacturers started offering new bells and whistles for their products once earlier concerns, such as capacity, timers, and defrosters, became commonplace. Servel boasted it had the only refrigerator to make ice cubes automatically and put them in a basket in 1953, while in 1955 Westinghouse was first with the Automatic Twin Juice Fountain, where two kinds of juice were on tap. By the mid 1950s many refrigerators were offering sliding or swing out shelves for easier access. In 1956, however, Hotpoint did them all one better by making the "world's biggest" swing-out door shelf, the Big-Bin. Swing-out shelves hit their zenith at the end of the decade with a GE model that was so sturdy it could hold

Sizzling Meals Broiled Right At Table!
(NO SMOKE, FUSS, FUMES !)

EXCLUSIVE HIDDEN-VENT DESIGN! A REAL SMOKELESS BROILER!

CHOICE OF HEATS- FOR COOKING, FOR SIMMERING

SPECIAL EASY-TO- CLEAN PLATE FOR DRIPPINGS

BROIL A WHOLE CHICKEN OR STEAK- 6 CHOPS-VEGETABLES-FISH- IN A JIFFY !

Manning Bowman
Means Best

25 bottles of milk. Although sliding shelves, separate freezer, and storage bins were offered by others, the Hotpoint Super-Stor refrigerator was the only brand to show Ricky Nelson and his brother David from TV's *Ozzie and Harriet* sitting on the floor, eating, in front of it.

Stove makers developed their share of innovations to attract new customers. The Kelvinator boasted "it cooks while no one looks," while Frigidaire offered a "thinking top" to eliminate the watching and waiting of cooking. Gibson stoves had an "Ups-a-Daisy" deep-well cooker for frying that featured a Numagic dial to raise it up from the stove's surface. Many stoves offered built-in broilers and pushbutton controls. But Hotpoint had all this, plus a deep-well fryer, in a range 30 inches wide. Their 39-inch Super-Deluxe model also included a built-in coffee maker and Rota-Grill barbecue; and even would call you with the melodic strains of the song "Tenderly" when the roast was done. For this stove, the term "Super-Deluxe" was not an exaggeration.

With all these new features, the kitchen became a comfortable zone in which to do chores and also a suitable space for family and friends to congregate and feel part of the activities. If a room offered push-button ease along with style and beauty, who would want to be excluded?

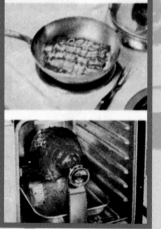

The heavy duty quality of most 1950s appliances was indicative of the value placed on the them by consumers. Even the smallest appliances, like toasters, irons, and mixers, were considered long-term investments to be used for years before replacement.

LOOK!
A REAL food
freezer!

Food Freezers are much-wanted appliances in America today! G.E. gives you a zero-degree freezer and a no-defrosting refrigerator in one cabinet!

Pick ONE cube
at a time!

Redi-Cube Ice Trays make it possible to pick out cubes singly, and return the rest—still in the dividers—to the refrigerator. Cubes will not drop out!

No more
defrosting!

Frost does not build up in the fresh-food section. Uncovered foods do not dry out! Foods remain crisp and fresh, in this General Electric Refrigerator.

No more
HARD butter!

Butter Conditioner mounted in the General Electric Refrigerator door keeps a full pound of butter at best temperature for mixing and spreading.

new! Amana

BUILT-IN FREEZERS AND REFRIGERATORS

STACK ONS

SIDE BY SIDE

With its compact size, Servel's 1953 Wonderbar refrigerator helped stretch the utility of refrigerators and became a popular addition for family rooms and built-in bars.

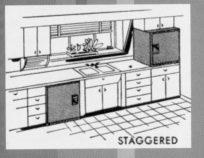

STAGGERED

CHECK YOUR KITCHEN

against this timesaving, work-saving ideal!

1. Sound-deadened steel construction; easy-gliding drawers, positive-closing doors.
2. Baked-on enamel finish—sparkles at the touch of a damp cloth.
3. Ample, accessible storage (including corner cabinet with shelves that turn, and rolling-door cabinet for spices)!
4. The greatest help you ever had with the revolutionary Youngstown Kitchens Jet-Tower Dishwasher.
5. One-piece, acid-resisting porcelain-enameled steel sink top with no-splash bowl.
6. Spacious, colorful, durable work surfaces of exclusive, clatter-proof Youngstown Kitchens Cusheen.
7. Quarter-Round Base What-Not adds attractive open storage for small appliances.
8. Improved Youngstown Kitchens Food Waste Disposer, 3 ways best, fits Electric or Cabinet Sink, abolishes garbage!

ENJOY the world's lightest work — brightest living — in the *only* kitchen with all these features!

Compare your present kitchen (or *any* kitchen) with this gleaming, efficient beauty. You'll want a Youngstown Kitchen!

You'll want its *baked-on* enamel finish that's so easy to clean and doesn't require painting; the rigid STEEL that won't buckle or warp.

You'll want the Youngstown Kitchens Food Waste Disposer, with continuous feed, longer life, thorough self-cleaning. And completely modernized dishwashing with the revolutionary Youngstown Kitchens Jet-Tower Dishwasher—its 58 swirling jets of booster-heated water brush-flush all parts of dishes in 9¾ minutes with exclusive *Hydro-Brush Action!*

Learn how easy it is to enjoy a Youngstown Kitchens Cabinet Sink that eases ⅔ of your kitchen work (13 models, with one-piece, acid-resisting porcelain-enameled steel tops); base and wall cabinets to give any kitchen roomy, accessible storage; work surfaces of exclusive, colorful Youngstown Kitchens Cusheen that's tough, long-lasting, and clatterproof.

Let your factory-trained Youngstown Kitchen dealer show you your dream kitchen in perfect miniature, how to save on installation and how easy it is to finance. If building, specify a Youngstown Kitchen. You'll save!

MULLINS MANUFACTURING CORPORATION
WARREN, OHIO
Youngstown Kitchens are sold throughout the World

This kitchen features revolutionary Youngstown Kitchens Electric Sink with Jet-Tower Dishwasher and Food Waste Disposer.

Youngstown Kitchens

Eight beautiful models to choose from !

The dishwasher traveled a long and circuitous path of development. First created around 1900 by Josephine Cochran, premium priced electric models appeared in 1912. Though fully enclosed models with rinse cycles were developed by 1940, popular acceptance of dishwashers was not achieved until the 1950s.

Sunbeam Corp. of Chicago, IL, introduced a new two-piece
vacuum coffeemaker designed by Alfonso Iannelli in 1939. The
basic design remained popular for over 20 years and could be
coupled with a matching tray and cream and sugar set.

Mixer Coffee Maker Iron Electric Comforter Griddle Waffle Baker Toaster

Only the Cycla-matic Frigidaire gives you all three

1

A real food freezer

Separate frozen storage for almost 50 lbs. of foods—frozen by *you* or bought when specials are most attractive. Cuts down shopping trips. Keeps fresh flavor locked in (safely for months, if you choose).

2

Defrosts itself

No controls to set. No pans to empty. Nothing to do or remember. Frigidaire's Cycla-matic Defrosting in the refrigerator compartment is completely automatic; banishes frost before it collects.

3

All the shelves roll out

No more treasure hunts on back shelves. Every shelf glides all the way out, brings the back to the front for easy picking. (All shelves are aluminum, too).

Compare Frigidaire! Compare the big freezer. Compare Cycla-matic Defrosting. Compare the roll-out shelves ... the Quick-ube ice trays, the simple, silent Meter-Miser mechanism that provides exactly the right cold levels through years and years of care-free service. Compare Frigidaire with any refrigerator!

More Frigidaire Refrigerators serve in more American homes than any other make

See your Frigidaire dealer. Look for his name in the Yellow Pages of your phone book, or write Frigidaire, Dept. 2134, Dayton 1, Ohio, for free folder. In Canada, Toronto 13, Ontario.

Cycla-matic Frigidaire

Built and backed by General Motors

Imperial Model IS-106

MAKE IT A WIFE-SAVER

Make it an all-steel kitchen!

Show any girl, from 18 to 80, a modern, custom-designed, all-steel kitchen . . . the kitchen that's a Wife-Saver . . . and watch what happens:

The all-steel kitchen brightens her eyes . . . because it's beautiful.

It lightens her heart . . . because it lightens her housework.

And it tickles her sense of thrift . . . because it's the most kitchen for the money there is.

A *steel* kitchen, remember. It has to be a *steel* kitchen. Because in the kitchen, as elsewhere, only steel can do so many jobs so well.

Steel gives you those smooth, easy-to-clean kitchen cabinets that open and shut so quietly, that adjust so readily to your storage needs, that can't possibly crack or come apart.

Steel gives you those strong, durable built-in conveniences: broom closet, mixer compartment, cutlery drawer, flour bin. And those smart, long-lasting accessories: breakfast bar, corner cabinet, kitchen desk. And that stainless counter edging that never needs polishing, never wears off.

And most important of all, steel gives you a colorful custom-made kitchen at ready-made cost. Because wall cabinets, base cabinets, counters, and accessories of steel are available as *standard, low-cost units* . . . top-notch quality at rock-bottom prices.

So make your kitchen a Wife-Saver . . . for beauty, for duty. See your local dealer today.

*Featured by
Mary Kay & Johnny on
The United States Steel Hour*

AMERICAN BRIDGE . . AMERICAN STEEL & WIRE and CYCLONE FENCE . . COLUMBIA-GENEVA STEEL
CONSOLIDATED WESTERN STEEL . . GERRARD STEEL STRAPPING . . NATIONAL TUBE . . OIL WELL SUPPLY
TENNESSEE COAL & IRON . . UNITED STATES STEEL PRODUCTS . . UNITED STATES STEEL SUPPLY
Divisions of UNITED STATES STEEL CORPORATION, PITTSBURGH
UNITED STATES STEEL HOMES, INC. . . UNION SUPPLY COMPANY
UNITED STATES STEEL EXPORT COMPANY . . UNIVERSAL ATLAS CEMENT COMPANY

Only STEEL can do so many jobs so well

UNITED STATES STEEL
USS

Marketing surveys in the mid-1950s indicated that women were playing an increased role in purchasing decisions for the household. With this in mind, many manufacturers began playing down mechanical qualities and increasing emphasis on convenience features.

General Electric's Toaster Oven from 1961 featured a glass window, a pop-up door, and a drawer. It was a convient way to heat meals and snacks and quickly became a 1960s kitchen staple.

For fine food and a festive table

Presto!

A modern electric oven that plugs in anywhere!

Two ways to look at a Bride

... if you want
WEDDING and SHOWER GIFTS
that will thrill her now
and help her later!

1 You can take the romantic view . . . and see her always as a lovely young bride. And Pyrex ware is one of the most popular gifts for brides. This handsome Pyrex cake dish is grand for baking, serving, and storing all kinds of food. Saves on dish-washing. Better give her at least a pair for layer cakes! Each, only . . . . **35¢**

2 You can take the practical view . . . and remember she'll have a hungry husband to feed. Even if she's a natural born cook you can't give her a more inspiring present than Pyrex ware. And she can watch foods cook. The Pyrex utility dish shown above should be in every bride's kitchen. Grand for roasts, chops, hot breads and cakes. Two sizes. Larger size, only . . **65¢**

THERE'S ONLY ONE
PYREX WARE

PYREX BRAND
OVEN WARE
for better and faster baking
CORNING GLASS WORKS
Corning, N. Y., U.S.A.

LOOK FOR THE FAMILIAR ORANGE LABEL
OR THIS TRADE-MARK PRESSED IN GLASS

Sunbeam's Model T-9 automatic toaster had an art deco-like, rounded top designed by George Scharfenberg in 1937. Patented as an "ornamental toaster," it served as a status symbol for housewives.

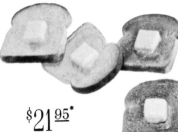

Toast the way YOU want it

... with G.E.'s NEW truly automatic toaster!

From light to dark—
and any shade
in between!

$21.95*

* Manufacturer's recommended
retail or Fair Trade price.

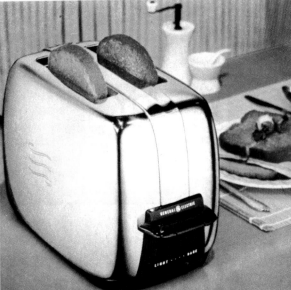

Charles Strite of Stillwater, MN, invented the pop-up toaster, with integral timer, in 1919 after being frustrated by burnt cafeteria toast. Seven years later his pop-up toaster was introduced as the "Toastmaster," and sales really took off after the introduction of pre-sliced Wonder Bread in 1930.

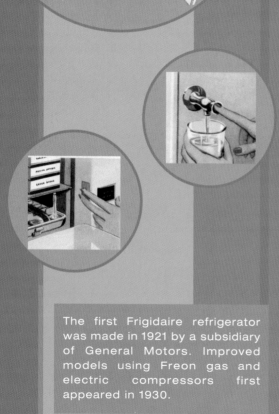

The first Frigidaire refrigerator was made in 1921 by a subsidiary of General Motors. Improved models using Freon gas and electric compressors first appeared in 1930.

SEE THE **NEW GIBSON**

WITH EXCLUSIVE NEW

Swing-out Servers

PLUS

Automatic Defrosting

It practically *hands* you the food . . . this beautiful new Gibson Refrigerator with "Swing-out Servers"! Meat locker, 2 crispers and shelf—they all swing right *to* you!

And oh lady, wait'll you see all the *other* wonders of this nothing-like-it Gibson! Automatic defrosting, big full-width freezer, door racks and butter storer —everything to make this the handiest, roomiest, most efficient refrigerator you ever dreamed of!

So don't miss seeing this new Gibson beauty with new "Cameo Cream" interior before you make your choice. Visit your Gibson dealer—*now!*

FREE! Accept this exciting

at your cooperating Gibson Dealer

3-bottle **Harriet Hubbard Ayer**

Cologne ACCORDION

For merely seeing a demonstration of the new Gibson refrigerator, electric range, food freezer or air conditioner at your cooperating Gibson Dealer! Offer limited! Act now!

. . . of course, it's electric! YOUR DOLLAR BUYS MORE THAN EVER BEFORE . . . WITH A

Gibson SINCE 1877

REFRIGERATORS • ELECTRIC RANGES • FREEZERS
AIR CONDITIONERS

©Gibson Refrigerator Co., Greenville, Mich.

In Canada—Gibson Refrigerator Company of Canada Limited, Montreal, Quebec.

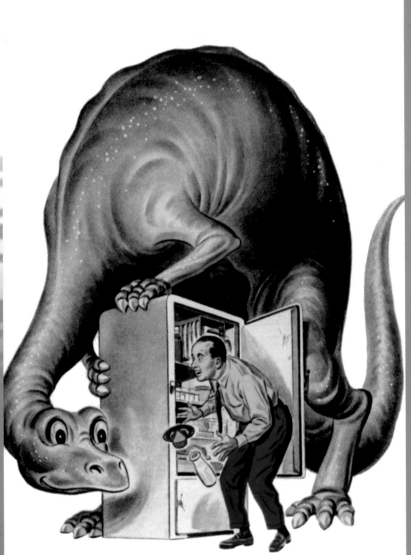

Is your refrigerator as outdated as a Dinosaur?

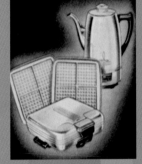

In 1910 Chester Beach rigged an electric motor to work with a food mixer on a stand, creating the first electric mixer for home use.

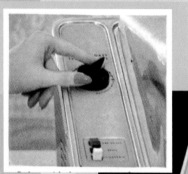

LOOK what you can do with a General Electric Rotisserie Oven...

It's a rotisserie...infra-red broiler...handy second ove

DUAL-PURPOSE
Guardian Service

a complete matched set of finest quality cooking and table service equipment

The easier way to cook . . .

Your reputation as a fine cook and a clever hostess is definitely established when you use GUARDIAN SERVICE. First, because you serve such delicious, taste-tempting and healthful foods . . . foods that look better . . . foods that are better . . . And it is so easily done, too. GUARDIAN SERVICE means *"waterless cooking"* . . . foods cooked in their own juices with more of the natural vitamins and minerals retained . . . with more of their full mouth-watering flavor.

And you're a clever hostess, too . . . your guests will admire your perfect meal that has been served direct-from-the-stove-to-the-table in the same

beautiful utensils in which it was prepared.

Yes, you'll get lasting pleasure from the complete GUARDIAN SERVICE. For breakfast, lunch, dinner or midnight snacks, there is a GUARDIAN SERVICE unit ready to help you . . . a complete matched set of "kitchen treasures" to provide you and your family with *all* the benefits of a definite and improved method of food preparation.

From the very moment you see the gleaming beauty, the exquisite design, the perfect, molded construction of GUARDIAN SERVICE, you will agree with thousands of home makers everywhere who say, "Here is a life-long friend."

A COMPLETE SET OF GUARDIAN SERVICE IN YOUR HOME WILL PROVIDE—

. . . the beautiful way to serve

Ronald Reagan stated "progress is our most important product" when he was a General Electric spokesman in the 1950s. Other celebrity spokespersons for kitchen product companies included actress Betty Furness for Westinghouse and Harriet Nelson, from TV's *Ozzie and Harriet*, for Hotpoint.

By the end of the 1950s push button controls had become commonplace on most kitchen appliances. A 1958 article in *Cosmopolitan*, "A Push Button Future," took the notion of push buttons a step further and predicted that by 1983 virtually every household or kitchen chore would be done effortlessly by simply pressing a button.

Your choice: 10¾" Covered Fry Pan (shown left), 8" Covered Fry Pan, 1½ qt., 2½ qt., and 3½ qt. Covered Sauce Pans.

*Patented

Hallite by
WEAR·EVER
ONLY WEAR·EVER HAS HALLITE

See Wear-Ever on the ALCOA "See It Now" television program—over CBS—
and on the new NBC-TV Daytime HOME Show—every week

THE ALUMINUM COOKING UTENSIL CO., NEW KENSINGTON, PENNA.

The most sensational cooking development in years... **CAPTIVE HEAT**

Exclusive with these Triple-Action Cooking Utensils of REYNOLDS *Lifetime* ALUMINUM

STEAM-TRAP LID — Steam is captured and held by the finely finished tongue-and-groove seal of the Steam-Trap Lid.

QUICK-CONDENSING WALL — Flavor is captured by the faster condensation on walls and lid—dripping back the juices, for "waterless" cooking at its best.

TRIPLE-THICK BOTTOM — Heat is captured, spread and held by the Triple-Thick Bottom — cooking evenly over the entire bottom area — no hot spots to scorch or burn.

Corning introduced their Flameware glass stovetop cookware in 1936, and it remained popular for over 20 years. Clear glass appealed to housewives, as it could be used for serving and storing as well as cooking. Metal bands kept the handles in place.

THE PERFECT GIFT FOR HIM OR HER !

K•M **Liquidizer**

Turns Fruits, Vegetables into Delicious Drinks,
Makes Frozen Daiquiris, Juleps,
Chops—Grinds—Grates—Purees—Whips!

My AMERICAN KITCHEN Saves Me
2 Hours a Day to Keep Myself Looking Young!

(...AND WE BOUGHT IT ON EASY FHA TERMS WITH 30 MONTHS TO PAY)

Start Your American Kitchen With
The "Mrs. America" Package Kitchen—Only $37 Down*

The "Mrs. America"
—Only $12.51 a month,
$369.95 complete* Includes: 54"
deluxe sink • Two 21" base cabinets† • Two
21" wall cabinets • Two what-not shelves.

A beautiful American Kitchen, with more work-saving features than *any* other kitchen in America will save you thousands of steps every day—hours of work. It will give you the freedom other women enjoy—time to do as you please.

Why wait? Now you can get the new complete "Mrs. America" package kitchen at a sensational money-saving price . . . or use it as a basic unit and add to it any way you wish. And the FHA terms with 30 months to pay make it so easy to get.

Ask Western Union Operator 25 for the name of your nearest dealer.

American KITCHENS

"SAVE 1000 STEPS A DAY"

American Central Division

AVCO

Connersville, Indiana

†Includes black tops; red tops available at slight extra cost.
*Prices and specifications subject to change without notice. FHA terms in effect at time advertising was prepared.

American Central Div., AVCO Mfg. Corp.
Connersville, Indiana, Dept. AH-8
Here's 25¢—rush me full color catalog showing kitchen layouts and planning book with miniature model kitchen cut-outs.

Name_____
Address_____
City_____ Zone____ State____

Prominent designer George Nelson designed the popular atomic clock for Herman Miller in 1949. Classroom models of molecules influenced the clock's spoke-and-ball design.

MIRRO-MATIC

the pressure pan that is changing the cooking customs of a nation...

You used to cook frozen veg...
from 8 to 10 minutes...
NOW they average only...
at 5 lbs. pressure...

A Kelvinator "Extra"
Big, Oversize Crispers

You used to boil or...

An exchange of household exhibits between the United States and the Soviet Union in 1959 created a setting for the famous "kitchen debates" between Vice President Richard Nixon and Soviet leader Nikita Krushchev. Nixon extolled the virtues of an American kitchen filled with modern appliances, while Krushchev, admittedly deficient in the domestic race, could only add that such automatic devices probably always malfunctioned.

sure control lets you choose the *right* pressure, then *automatically* prevents pressure from going higher than your recipe requires . . . 5, 10, or 15 lbs. *You can hear* it as it goes about its work, speeding, protecti... ...rting your cooking, while *you* relax a... ...it!

What to Look F... ...IRRO-MATIC

When you're sel... ...ur MIRRO-MATIC at the store, notice its V... ...oprene gasket, so easy to re- move, clean, and ... See how simply the cover opens and closes, ...liding the handles apart or together. See the... ...y domed shape of the cover . . . that's to giv... ...pace for bulky foods, to let you use its *full cap...* ...canning as well as cooking.

Choose the siz... ...st fits your *immediate* needs. You can always a... ...er, when you need it. And, that way, you'll ... ...e pleasures and benefits that are waiting for you in MIRRO-MATIC ... the pressure pan that is changing the cooking customs of a nation!

ALUMINUM GOODS MFG. CO., MANITOWOC, WIS.
World's Largest Manufacturer of Aluminum Cooking Utensils

At last !
a **Freezer** Tailor-Made
for Your **Kitchen**
Manitowoc Sub-zero

"COOL" COOKING IN GLASS

In new **electronic** ranges . . .

food will be cooked in **seconds** . . .

right in its original Owens-Illinois **glass** container!

The Sperry Hutchinson Co. began distributing S&H trading stamps in 1896. Customers received the stamps with other purchases and redeemed them later for household wares. By 1960, S&H stamps led the competition and were offered at thousands of retail outlets. Trading stamps lost favor in the 1970s when stores started discounting prices to attract customers.

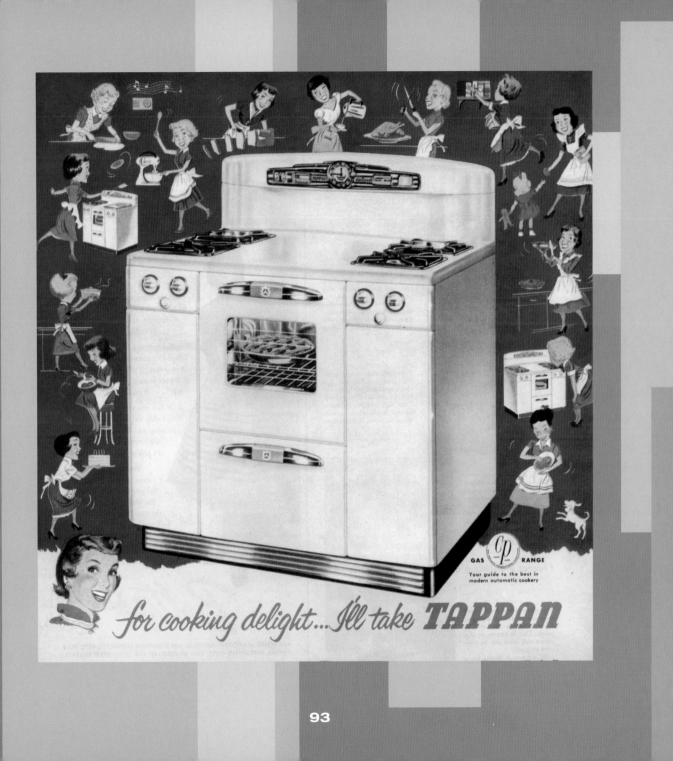

for cooking delight... I'll take **TAPPAN**

Food storage and preservation were still tricky for the postwar housewife, but Tupperware arrived to lend a hand. The key to Tupperware's marketing success was its home party plan. A 1950s Tupperware party booklet included a game where participants sculpted a piece of chewed gum and earned a prize for the best design.

And they cooked happily ever after !

Frigidaire's streamlined Sheer Look appliances from the late 1950s were first shown in their 1956 Kitchen of Tomorrow display. The design had a high fashion influence and was a popular success. Its angular look continues to influence kitchen appliances today.

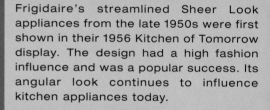

GREAT NEW KITCHEN IDEA!

the *Decorator Refrigerator*

by International Harvester

Revolutionary new idea enables you to make your refrigerator a feature
of your kitchen decoration. Match it with your curtains—blend it with your
color scheme. Use any pattern—any color fabric you choose. And you
can change it as often as you change your mind!

*a Fashion First
exclusive with*

INTERNATIONAL HARVESTER

INTERNATIONAL HARVESTER

The Quick-Meal Secret of 22 Million Cooks Goes Automatic!

New Presto *Electric* Pressure Cooker

AUTOMATICALLY **controls heat**
AUTOMATICALLY **controls pressure**
AUTOMATICALLY **vents air**

Cooks 3 times faster, saves vitamins and flavor!

Busy as you are, you needn't be just a "weekend cook." With a Presto Electric Pressure Cooker, you can fix a rich variety of "Sunday" menus any day of the week, electrically, because your Presto does an hour's cooking in 20 minutes!

There's no watching or waiting. Just set the Sweep Heat Selector, and your Presto Electric Pressure Cooker vents air automatically, keeps heat and pressure where you want it. It keeps flavor where you want it, too — inside the food. Saves vitamins and minerals; actually brightens colors.

Twenty-two million cooks count on Presto Cookers for better meals in less time; for healthier family menus every day. Now their secret is yours — electrically — for only **$29.95***

*Manufacturer's recommended retail or Fair Trade Price. Fed. Tax Incl.

Serves up food
3 times faster

	PRESTO TIME	OLD TIME
Pot Roast (4 lbs.)	30 minutes	2 hours
Picnic Ham (4 lbs.)	30 minutes	2 hours
Spare Ribs (2 lbs.)	15 minutes	1½ hours
Swiss Steak	15 minutes	1½ hours
Beef Stew	15 minutes	1½ hours
Vegetable Soup	20 minutes	2 hours
Chicken (3 to 4 lbs.)	15 minutes	2 hours
Whole Potatoes (med.)	10 minutes	35 minutes
Hubbard Squash	15 minutes	45 minutes
Carrots	3 minutes	25 minutes
Custard	3 minutes	35 minutes

Tupperware became popular in the 1950s with its line of pastel storage bowls and accessories. Its design proved that lightness, translucency, and flexibility could be assets rather than faults. Early advertising boasted the product as "the miracle on your pantry shelf."

The Toastmaster toaster was promoted in 1951 as "part of the family . . . a cherished possession for which no substitute is ever completely satisfying."

The amazing food freezer that actually <u>makes room</u> for itself in any kitchen!

new ⟶ **REVCO DINETTE**

it's a big food freezer!

it's a drop-leaf table, too!

FEATURING

Revcold

FASTEST FREEZING ACTION

The revolutionary Revco Dinette has all these advanced features:

- Two drawer, 180 lb. capacity
- All-aluminum freezing compartment
- Convenient foot pedal door control
- Ample seating for average family
- Double-duty laminated plastic top
- Choice of beautiful color combinations
- Matching chairs available

Now, from Revco, a size-right, style-right beauty that makes easy freezer living possible in any size kitchen. Food storage and serving are effectively combined in a single unit for step-and-space-saving. Baked enamel cabinet; gleaming, scratch-resistant plastic table top. Both in magnificent colors. Visit your Revco dealer or write for free literature. See how the Revco Dinette Freezer will serve most efficiently as your family food center.

Be sure to see these other famous Revco Freezers:

Chests Uprights Bilt-ins

Revco

FOOD FREEZERS

REVCO, INC., Deerfield, Michigan

ROTO-BROIL "400" King-Size Fiesta

all for less than the price of Roto-Broil alone!*

For over 25 years Raymond Loewy commuted regularly from New York to Dayton, OH, to develop kitchen appliances for Frigidaire. He preferred simple designs that were easy to clean and were free of superfluous details. Many of his ideas retain their popularity and fresh look today.

Advertisements for appliances in the early years of the twentieth century invariably showed appliances being used by maids rather than the lady of the house. Postwar America addressed its growing middle class by creating more affordable household appliances.

AUTOMATIC! Every pan you own acts like a costly automatic saucepan, on the famous Gas Burner-with-a-Brain*. Minds itself. The thermostat holds the cooking temperature you set—so food won't scorch or boil over!

"SEE-LEVEL" BROILING! Now the best way to broil is the most convenient! You can see, you can supervise . . . and yet, because it's Gas, you still broil with the broiler-door shut . . . neither you nor your kitchen get overheated!

ROPER

Microwave cooking was discovered in the 1940s, and the first oven was marketed as a "Radarange" that sold for $3000. Further refinements and price cuts in the 1950s and 1960s led to increased consumer acceptance in the 1970s; in 1975 over one million microwave ovens were sold.

SET IT— AND FORGET IT...

your new KELVINATOR "AUTOMATIC COOK" ELECTRIC RANGE

In 1958 Corning announced the discovery of Pyroceram, a durable ceramic-glass material impervious to heat and cold. It was featured in a line of ceramic cookware that was popular throughout the 1960s.

ONLY $24⁹⁵

MAKES 8 FULL CUPS

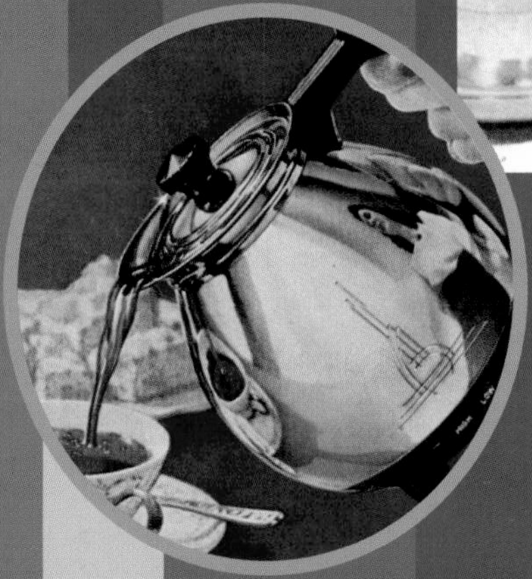

The Hotpoint brand first gained access to America's households in the early 1900s with its electric "hot point" iron. A heating element ran the length of the iron and met at the point to create a full surface of heat. Hotpoint later expanded on its success with other quality appliances for the kitchen and elsewhere.

Vacuum Cleaner · Tank Cleaner · Water Heater · Range · Home Freezer · Laundromat · Dryer · Cabinets · Comforter · Mixer · Coffee Maker · Fan · Iron · Waffle Baker · SUPERB NEW TWO-TEMP REFRIGERATOR · Roaster Oven · Hot Plate · Toaster · Waste-Away · Cozy Glow · Cleaner

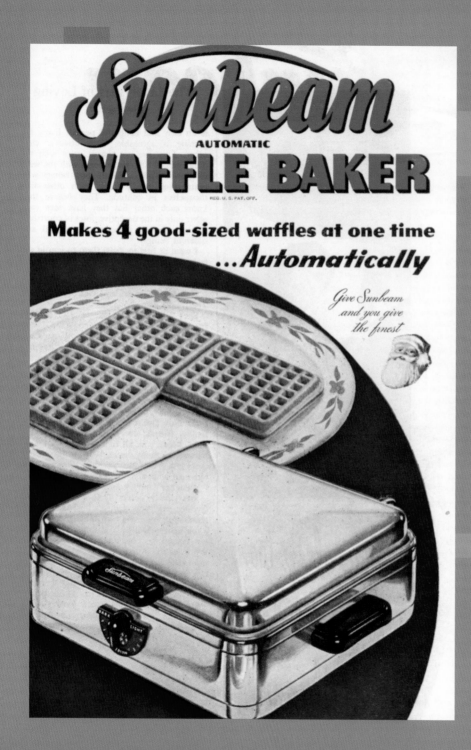

Sunbeam
AUTOMATIC
WAFFLE BAKER
REG. U. S. PAT. OFF.

Makes 4 good-sized waffles at one time
...Automatically

Give Sunbeam and you give the finest

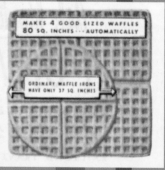

MAKES 4 GOOD SIZED WAFFLES
80 SQ. INCHES · · · AUTOMATICALLY

ORDINARY WAFFLE IRONS
HAVE ONLY 37 SQ. INCHES

The Cory electrical knife sharpener was designed by Joseph Palma, Jr. in 1947. Its deluxe styling competed well with the higher priced models from other companies.

Two ovens and broiler at reach-in height

Surface units that let you see into pans

All cooking controls at eye-level

Cutting board right where you need it

. . or surrounded by storage units to look "built-in."

Parisian Marc Gregoire perfected a method for applying non-sticking PolyTetraEthylene (PTFE) to aluminum cookware in 1956. First marketed as T-Fal, it was a runaway success when introduced to the American marketplace as Teflon in 1960.

Permanent G-E Alnico magnet on refrigerator door provides silent, automatic closing . . . seals effectively.

Foot pedal opens freezer door at the touch of your toe. Leaves both hands free for carrying foods.

-14N. Available in Mix-or-Match Colors: Canary Yellow, Turquoise Green, Petal Pink, Cadet Blue, Woodtone Brown—or White. Your choice of either right- or left-han

14-cubic-foot General Electric Refrigerator-Freezer has Revolving Shelves . . . Magnetic Safety Door

of course . . .
I used my KitchenAid!

Saves so much time! And results are so much better, when you stir, whip, blend . . . with a *KitchenAid!* *KitchenAid's* big revolving single beater travels 'round and 'round inside the bowl, thoroughly mixing *all* ingredients. Attachments, too, for every kitchen task. See *KitchenAid,* "the finest made," at better dealers everywhere, or write *KitchenAid* Electric Housewares Div., Dept. KB, The Hobart Manufacturing Co., Troy, Ohio. In Canada: 175 George St., Toronto 2.

KitchenAid
The Finest Made . . . by *Hobart*

In the early part of the twentieth century, Albert Marsh discovered that nichrome, an alloy of nickel and chrome, glowed red and heated without disintegrating. His discovery led to the first practical electric heaters and toasters.

See "The Patrice Munsel Show" — on TV

GM GOLDEN ANNIVERSARY

Frigidaire – Built and Backed by General Motors

Model RCI-75-58

A WOMAN'S WONDER SINK

ELKAY
Lustertone

garbage wrappings and toting...
unsightly, unsanitary garbage cans...

You'll love the
Westinghouse
FOOD WASTE
disposer

GADGETS AND ACCESSORIES

3

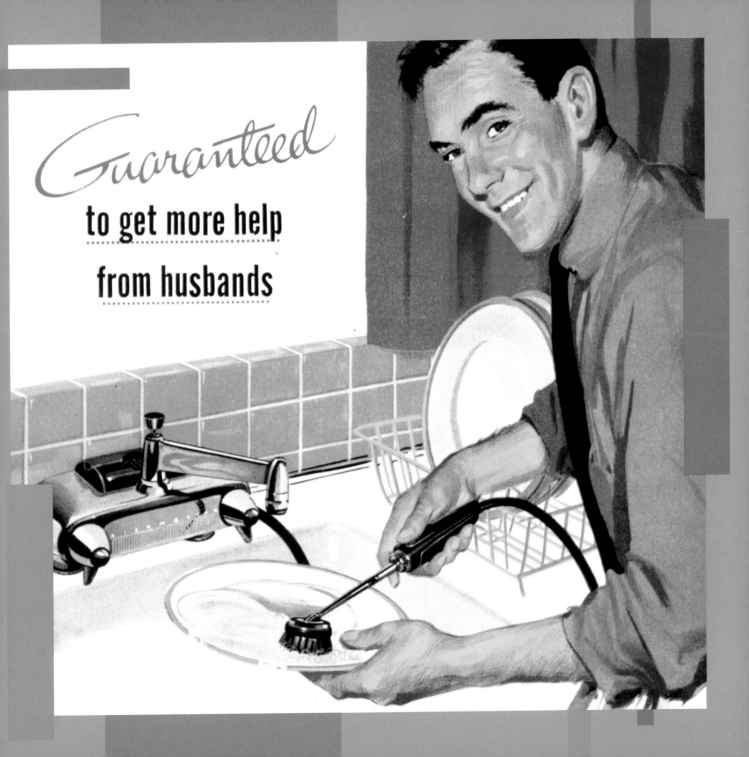

The seemingly endless assortment of kitchen gadgets available to housewives in the 1950s was a culmination of more than 100 years of developments. In the first part of the 1800s a basic set of kitchen utensils might include cooking pots, pans, ladles, knives, forks, spoons, and a few other utensils. Simple rolling pins and food strainers were among the few specialized tools. Cooking methods were usually handed down from mother to daughter and among a close circle of individuals with little contact to outside information. Such informal communication channels were slow to promote advances. Early cookbooks even omitted ingredient measurements, as this information wasn't considered critical for cooks with years of experience.

Yankee peddlers who sold kitchen wares from town to town acted as early catalysts for change, offering a wide range of products and demonstrating the advantages of new ones. Homemakers quickly adopted egg beaters, peelers, and other kitchen gadgets, which were a decided improvement over using basic utensils such as a bowl and spoon for beating ingredients. Another wave of influence came with the widespread popularity of mail-order catalogs in the late 1800s, where caption writers effectively communicated options for buyers and touted the features of deluxe models.

After basic kitchen needs were satisfied, housewives became more receptive to trying new and improved gadgets. This interest furthered advances in kitchen-preparation items throughout the first decades of the twentieth century. Egg beaters, whippers, peelers, sifters, and other products benefited from advances in metal plating and other manufacturing processes. Even everyday items like bowls or spoons were likely to be replaced by new versions offering a more durable finish or other benefit.

America's First and Only Folding Buffet Server!

Fold-Away BUFFET

Pat. Appd. For

BEAUTIFUL, GIANT BUFFET SERVER THAT FOLDS COMPACTLY FOR EASY STORING

Automobiles and better roads in the 1920s led to increased mobility for consumers, more access to stores, and a greater emphasis on product merchandising. Sellers began offering a wider assortment of peelers, scoops, cheese slicers, pastry crimpers, and other kitchen gadgets and also began putting them on display with placards to illustrate their use. A number of companies prospered by specializing in gadgets, including the Acme Co. in New Jersey and Thurnauer & Sons in New York City. By the 1930s and 1940s, stores started setting aside special "gadget" sections, increasing the profile and awareness of the category. Manufacturers responded to this demand by creating colorful packaging and store displays to promote sales.

In the 1950s new and improved kitchen gadgets addressed the issue of convenience and ease of use for housewives. Much of the appeal of these products was their ability to win you over with added features. Packaging claims and illustrations became important point-of-purchase sales tools. An easier and neater to use gadget might be called "no fuss and no muss," while simple plastic pie containers could "keep pie tasty fresh." Advanced gadgets including choppers, juicers, cookie guns, French fry cutters, etc. went one step beyond simple devices to give easier and faster results. Electric helpers like the "amazing" Peel King were "wife savers" that would do the peeling and paring work for you.

Large gadget companies actively promoted a wide assortment of products. Ekco products in Chicago made just about every kind of gadget known, including a dizzying array of can openers. From simple hand held units to basic and deluxe wall models and top-of-the-line electric versions, there was a can opener for every budget, similar to the breadth of price range in cars. The multitude of 1950s convenience gadgets was joined by a host of others that would add zest to your meal preparation or extend the range of your kitchen prowess. These included numerous cake molds and decorators, garnishers, sandwich toasters, ravioli makers,

Christmas calls for Cookies...

make pretty ones, quickly, and fancy pastries too,

with the

MIRRO

Cooky and Pastry Press

It's fun to make fancy cookies and pastries with this practical press.
Just fill it with dough and turn the knob to form perfect cookies
right on your cooky sheet, ready for the oven! Your choice of a dozen
shapes, and you can make up to 80 beauties without stopping
to refill. Using the pastry-making attachments you can form eclairs,
lady fingers, meringue shells and cream puffs almost as quickly.
What if fancy cookies and pastries *are* 60c . . . 90c . . . $1.20 a dozen
in the shops? *Your* family can have them and you can
have the fun of making them . . . for pennies! . . . with the
MIRRO Cooky and Pastry Press.

ALUMINUM GOODS MANUFACTURING COMPANY • MANITOWOC, WISCONSIN
WORLD'S LARGEST MANUFACTURER OF ALUMINUM COOKING UTENSILS

Get **MIRRO** at department, hardware,
and housefurnishing stores, wherever
dealers sell the finest aluminum.

CREAM PUFFS

MERINGUE SHELLS

ECLAIRS

LADY FINGERS

FANCY COOKIES

122

and even a French waffle maker for your toaster. Many of these specialized "needs" for the kitchen were practically unheard of previously but were now available for the discriminating housewife.

Other products developed for the kitchen of the 1950s fell into a distinctly miscellaneous category. Amusing figural salt and pepper shakers, spice dispensers, and countless other accessories might not have addressed urgent needs but certainly made your kitchen experience more enjoyable. What benefit did a plastic, wind-up "helping hand" have? It was strictly open to question.

The gadgets available in the 1950s led many housewives down a path of heightened awareness. There was a multitude of choices in color and quality levels unlike anything merchandising had seen before. Packaging with perky graphics and boldly stated claims became impromptu salesmen trying to catch the attention of shoppers. New kitchen gadgets advertised by televised pitchmen sometimes took their message to unexpected levels. In a mid-1950s commercial, Popeil's Chop-O-Matic food chopper showed you more diced up vegetables than you would probably use at a large banquet. While the "Automatic" Potato Peeler from another marketer could wash and peel with "no work and no waste" and also "clean itself." With such miraculous gadgets as these at hand, you were truly led to believe that other wonders in the future, including atomic kitchens, would be just around the corner.

Sweet Music

♪ Color stays bright...no polishing ever ♪

I'm so thrilled with the sparkling magic of Hallite's striking beauty and quality that I bring them right to the table. The rich, copper-toned covers will keep their lustre forever—and without polishing! Hallite utensils make cooking so easy, too, because they're made of special, thick aluminum that spreads heat fast and evenly. Foods won't scorch or stick, because most cooking can be done over low heat. And lovely leaf hangers are included free, so that pans and covers can be hung in attractive wall arrangements. So why don't you visit your nearest store and make your choice from the complete line of Hallite. They're sold individually or in attractive sets, all modestly priced.

Home, home on the range

Hallite by **WEAR-EVER**

WEAR-EVER
ALL ALUMINUM
TRADE MARK
HALLITE

COOKING UTENSIL CO., INC., NEW KENSINGTON, PA.

Hallite aluminum cookware was a premium line from Wear-Ever in the 1950s. It featured deluxe gold-toned lids and aluminum handles on its pans, and its teakettle utilized an elongated handle as elegant as it was functional.

124

SUPERWHIRL

the finest smoothest operating beater ever made

SUPER PACKAGING

Individually packed in a beautiful gift box with plenty of eye appeal.

Only **3 95** LIST
East of the Rocky Mountains

SUPER DESIGN

Beautifully streamlined with bright chrome finish. Moulded plastic handle and knob in red, green or popular new yellow.

SUPER CONSTRUCTION

Rugged, die-cast construction with stainless steel structural support essential to lifetime wear.

SUPER SMOOTH OPERATION

Die-cast gears for positive quiet operation at slow or high speeds. Will not slip.

SUPER VALUE

Nothing has been overlooked to make this the finest beater value in every way . . . yet it is popularly priced.

Turner & Seymour Co. produced an egg beater model called the Superwhirl to upgrade their standard model, the Bluewhirl. Most larger gadget companies marketed several egg beaters to satisfy the needs of every buyer. Deluxe models had stainless steel blades and heavy-duty construction.

The Rival Coffee-Mill was a fancy wall-mounted unit designed to coordinate with other Rival kitchen aids. It had a heavy-duty grinding mechanism and an attached clear plastic container that made it an unusual addition for the 1950s kitchen.

New Rival COFFEE-MILL*

PAYS FOR ITSELF IN THE FLAVOR IT SAVES!

CASH IN on Present High Coffee Costs

Choice of Red, White, or Yellow
$9.95*
All Chrome Model
$10.95*

Here's the new, beautiful appliance every woman wants—to serve her family finer coffee—and also save money. Rival COFFEE-MILL will more than pay its way because *FRESH* grinding means using *less* coffee for each cup because the rich FULL-BODIED flavor is retained only in the whole bean...and buying whole coffee beans costs less, often ten cents per pound less!

Rival COFFEE-MILL adjusts to any grind from coarse to fine, and it's easy to use because each bean is cracked before it is ground ... the ball-bearing handle turns the individually fitted abrasive-resistant chrome nickel grinding burrs swiftly, smoothly...and it's the perfect gift idea for 1951!

FITS RIVAL WALL BRACKET

Pressing button on either side releases graduated, transparent, measuring cup.

1. Vacuum Pot   3. Percolator
2. Drip Pot   4. Open Pot

Handy selector dial sets Rival COFFEE-MILL for any grind.

Revolutionary Rival Grinding Principle! Feed screw cracks each coffee bean before reaching grinding burrs—smoother, easier, quieter grinding.

Can-O-Mat   Juice-O-Mat   Steam-O-Matic   Shred-O-Mat

Rival MANUFACTURING COMPANY
Kansas City, Mo.
★ TRADE MARK   * Subject to change without notice
Rival Manufacturing Co. of Canada, Ltd., Montreal

Rival created an entire line of kitchen gadgets using the "O-Mat" name in the 1940s and 1950s. Along with popular can openers and ice crushers, they also produced a Juice-O-Mat, Slice-O-Mat, Grind-O-Mat, and even a Jar-O-Mat that opened jars. The products featured durable metal and plastic construction and were available in a variety of colors.

127

128

BLUE MAGIC

KRISPY KAN

The Moisture Absorbing Canister

THIS MAGIC KNOB ABSORBS MOISTURE

Retail Price
$1.95

We consulted your customers, the American housewife, on every detail of this product and in every case the response was overwhelmingly favorable.

REPLACEMENT OR A REFUND OF MONEY
Guaranteed by Good Housekeeping
IF NOT AS ADVERTISED THEREIN

Krispy Kan keeps foods crisp and tasty

BLUE MAGIC, the most unique line in the housewares field, now introduces its new product... KRISPY KAN. It fulfills a startling guarantee to keep crackers, potato chips, pretzels and many other foods, crisp and tasty at all times. Individually packaged, it is shipped in a specially made container and eliminates awkward wrapping problems. Nothing like KRISPY KAN has ever been on the market before. It has an immediate appeal to housewives ... is durably constructed ... beautifully finished ... and the retail price is ideal for volume sales. **Nationally Advertised ... Free Promotions and Displays**

MANUFACTURED BY LUCE MANUFACTURING CO. • GROTON, VERMONT

C-90

FOR FULL DETAILS ON *KRISPY KAN* **FILL OUT COUPON ON THE REVERSE SIDE** ▶

To prolong freshness, Krispy Kan Canisters offered a built-in absorbing element to help remove moisture from crackers, cookies, and other dry foods.

The Trig Singing Tea Kettle from West Bend added bright hues in colored aluminum and whistled better than the ordinary teakettle. It was noisy and brash, and housewives loved it!

Trimz was one of several ready-made borders available for housewives in the 1940s and 1950s looking to add a decorative edge to their kitchen shelves or cabinets. Border edging fell out of favor when the clean lines of modern design took hold.

MIRRO
THE FINEST ALUMINUM

Your Best Buy

MIRRO-MATIC ACCESSORIES

TWINSET PANS

MIRRO COVERED MOLD

MINUTE MINDER

If a cook had limited burners or scarce time to work, Mirro Twinset Pans provided a convenient shortcut. The pans allowed two different foods to boil at once in the same pan.

NEW! "Plasti-Chrome" beauty for your kitchen—

"Apple Clusters" on shelves

You've never seen such color-beauty for your kitchen before—new "Plasti-Chrome" Royledge is brighter, sparkling with color, stronger. In minutes, for pennies, you'll make your kitchen a "garden of color" by placing gay Royledge on all shelves. So easy, simply place on shelf and fold down the decorative doubl-edge. Pick your favorite Royledge pattern now at 5 & 10's, naborhood, hardware, dept. stores.

Plasti-Chrome
Royledge
Shelving Paper and Edging all-in-one
9 ft. and
24 ft. pkgs.

Royal Lace Paper Works, Inc., Bklyn.
Td. Mk. "Royledge" Reg. U. S. Pat. Off.

EASY TO USE
TRIMZ
TRADE MARK
READY-PASTED BORDERS
GAY!
COLORFUL!
INEXPENSIVE!

CHERRY CIDER—Zestful color for "culinary workshops"

CHEF & MAID—This jolly couple enlivens kitchens

LOTUS BLOSSOM—Lovely pastel charm for bathrooms

SPRING RIPPLE—For the bathroom that calls for color

BLUE GLORY—Ideal for living, dining or bedroom

ROSEBUD—A piquant pattern for bedroom

Bright new ideas for crowded cupboards

Rubbermaid
of course

Modernize your cupboard space with these brand new Rubbermaid ideas . . . bright, practical, durable!

CUSHION YOUR SHELVES WI[...]
Smart, new **Rubbermaid Shelf-K[...]** you permanent, silencing shelf [...] Ribbed to keep glassware fron [...] Molded with special plate rail f [...] dishes. Ready-sized for your cabi[...]

PLATE AND CUP STORING MA[...]
No more bothersome stacking [...] **Rubbermaid Plate Racks** and **Rubb[...] Racks** prevent chip[...] cup wonderfully ea[...]

GOOD NEWS FO[...]
A clever, comp[...] **Saucer Rack** to hold [...] each cup in its own [...] Prevents breaking [...] . . . and it's portab[...]

Stove Mats—$.79-$2.49

Rectangular Wastebaskets—$1.49-$4.98

Round Wastebaskets—$1.19-$2.98

Heavy Duty Bucket—$1.98

Dinnerware Rack—$3.98

Drainer Trays—$2.69-$2.98

Dish Drainers—$2.29-$3.98

Twin Sink Divider Mat—$1.69

Sink Mats—$1.29-$2.49

Dish Pans—$.98-$1.98

Laundry Basket—$3.98

Covered Container-Diaper Pail—$4.98

Storage Bin—$2.49 each
Two Bins Illustrated

Door Mats—$.98-$6.98

Tissue Dispenser—$1.79
Toilet Top Tray—$1.49

Rubbermaid got its start making rubber dust pans and rubber-coated, wire dish drainers in the 1930s and 1940s. In the 1950s their expanded product line made it easy for housewives to color coordinate kitchen accessories.

Quart size Shaker for
drinks or juices....59¢

Smart Bread Box, keeps
bread fresher....1.29

for your
kitchen and
refrigerator

new **PLASTICS** ideas
to lighten your
chores and
brighten your
Home!

Yes, plastic housewares . . . made of STYRON . . . give
modern housewives plenty of time for leisure. Handy, convenient for storing or serving—from refrigerator to table
without using unnecessary dishes. Note too how the new "soft tone"
colors add a fresh decor to your kitchen or table setting.

for your
table

MADE OF
STYRON
A DOW PLASTIC

Handy 2½-qt. Pitcher;
asstd. colors........98¢

High dome Cake Cover
on 11½" Tray....1.98

Quart size Shaker for
drinks or juices....59¢

Smart Bread Box, keeps
bread fresher....1.29

3-pc. Refrig. Set....98¢
Individual jars: 25¢, 49¢

4-pc. Canister Set, mod-
ern design....Set, 2.98

4-pc. Tumbler Set in
asstd. colors....Set, 39¢

Knife and Fork Tray, 3
sizes....59¢, 79¢, 98¢

Attractive 5-pc. Salad
'n Snack Set......1.49

Flavor Server Set for
relish, sauces, etc...98¢

Salt 'n Pepper Set,
range size....Set 49¢

Attractive Creamer 'n
Sugar Tray Set....98¢

for home
decoration

Modern design watering
can, 14-oz. size....49¢

Spinning Wheel Planter 98¢
African Violet Flower Pot *49¢
Flower Pot with Saucer*, in 4
sizes...25¢, 35¢, 49¢ & 59¢
(*As illustrated in use)

Buy all your plastic needs at
your nearby ... **BEN FRANKLIN**
SCOTT or **BUTLER BROTHERS** store

BEN FRANKLIN   SCOTT   BUTLER BROTHERS

BUTLER BROTHERS
Headquarters in Chicago

Flavor Server Set for
relish, sauces, etc...98¢

Attractive Creamer 'n
Sugar Tray Set....98¢

Attractive 5-pc. Salad
'n Snack Set......1.49

Salt 'n Pepper Set,
range size.....Set 49¢

Handy 2½-qt. Pitcher;
asstd. colors.......98¢

Quart size Shaker for
drinks or juices....59¢

3-pc. Refrig. Set....98¢
Individual jars: 25¢, 49¢

Swift offers you this amazing
Sandwich Toaster

RETAIL VALUE, $1.00

YOURS FOR ONLY **50¢**

with number copied from top of any can of Swift's Premium Canned Meats

Marvelous for picnics, barbecues, camp-outs! Swell for fireplace frolics. Indispensable for everyday kitchen use. Get several.

Swift makes this remarkable offer to acquaint you with the newest Swift's Premium Canned Meats— Chopped Ham, Hamburgers, Pork Sausage and Frankfurts. Try them *all* in your new Sandwich Toaster.

Toasts delicious sandwiches of *every* kind on top of range, hot plate, or over open fire. Hurry— summer time is picnic time!

Goes in like this

Comes out like this

y this Prem and Cheese sandwich

Swift's Premium *Canned Meats*

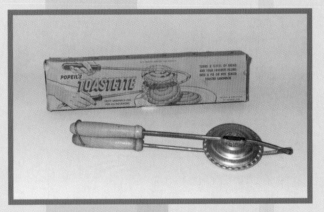

The Toas-Tite sandwich pie maker was a faddish 1950s cooking gadget where users put cheese, meat, or leftovers between two slices of bread in the unit and held it over a stove to create a compact, toasted sandwich.

Without its packaging, the Citra Grapefruit Corer is a mysterious, post-digger-type device with odd wood handles. It is a good example of mid-twentieth century gadgetry created to serve a very specific purpose.

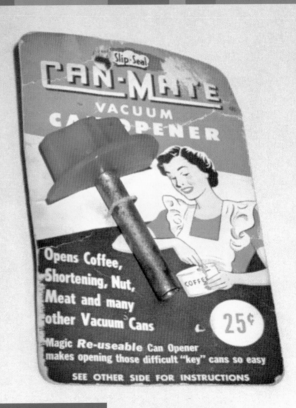

The Can-Mate can opener provided additional leverage when opening troublesome, key-wound, tin vacuum cans. Key-wound cans were used on coffee, shortening, and peanut cans for many years.

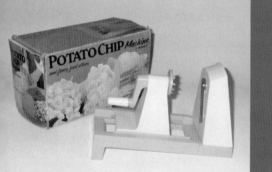

Neat and convenient, the Lustro-Ware Cheese Slicer stored and sliced boxed cheese in its handy plastic container.

Sea Food Shell
WAFFLE MOLD

HIRCO

MADE OF CAST ALUMINUM

- fun for serving
- simple to make
- easy to use

- Scrambled Eggs with Bacon
- Vegetable Melody
- Fricassees
- Chop Suey with Rice
- Au Gratin Dishes
- Ala King Dishes
- Tarts

SEA FOOD PLATES (Shown above "Shrimp C...

SALADS SUNDAES FRUIT MOLDS VEGETABLE

On shelves at left (and above), "Rose o' Day" pattern

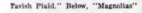

Tavish Plaid." Below, "Magnolias"

SALADS

FRUIT MOLDS

FRUIT MOLDS

141

NOW Decorate your Kitchen for Pennies!

STARTING APRIL 20, see Royledge Carnival of New Spring Patterns at local stores

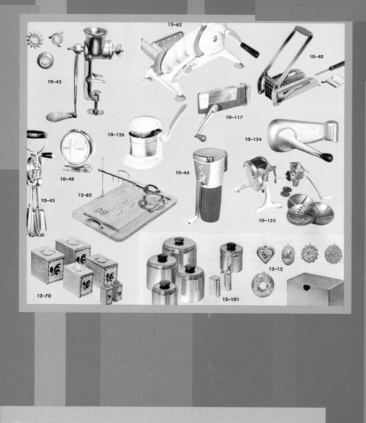

The Veg-O-Matic, introduced by Popeil in 1961, used a rapid-fire TV presentation to demonstrate its time-saving features. This approach was necessary to accommodate the Federal Communication Commission's new two-minute limit for commercials. Previous kitchen gadget ads had more time for detail.

... and learn all about flavor!

...nough to go around!

PEAS are rich, buttery peas . . .
...by-tender skins. Picked just when
...ne-sweet goodness is at its peak. Rushed
...ld to tin within an average of 2 hours, to
...their sunny flavor for you.

CORN, whole kernel and cream style, has that
...fresh delicacy. Grown from plump, special
...that have taken Libby years to perfect.

...say—to learn all about flavor, give Libby's a whirl!

Libby, McNeill & Libby, Chicago 9, Ill.

Libby's **CORN**

Libby's **PEAS**

Aunt Jemima Pancakes offered numerous cooking gadget premiums throughout the 1950s and 1960s. The Parti-Pan-Caker, available by mail in the early 1960s, made it easy to form pancakes into animal shapes and gave kids another excuse to play with their food.

"Look what mommy made with Aunt Jemima's new PARTI-PAN-CAKER!"

1. Place Parti-Pan-Caker on griddle.
Preheat mold for about 20 seconds.

2. Pour batter into Parti-Pan-Caker.
Bake pancakes until edges look cooked.

3. Lift Parti-Pan-Caker from griddle.
Turn pancakes; bake other side.

Dairies often used the Speed-E Whipper as a promotional item, maximizing on its keen ability to whip and mix their products.

One of many specialty pan sets, the Creamo Checker Board Cake Pan cleverly created a checker board cake using light and dark batters.

Blue Streak No. A-349-1

Flint No. 891

Zim-matic No. Z-12M

Magna-matic

Open cans blindfolded!

Best No. 170

Flex Roll Champion

Magic Hostess No. 5311

Dazey No. 88AC

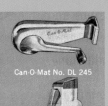

Can-O-Mat No. DL 245

A yellow tomato was created to accompany the Squeezit Catsup Dispenser, though it had more to do with novelty than mustard.

A New Era in Cooking

(Begins on page 102)

WHAT DOES IT DO?

It watches your food for you and automatically regulates the fuel supplied to the element. Once the selected temperature is reached, the heat source is cut off. When the temperature starts to fall below your selected setting, the sensing element in the center of the surface element registers the lowered temperature and heat is renewed as needed to maintain constant, even heat throughout the cooking process. No danger of fats overheating and smoking—no danger of violent boiling destroying valuable vitamins and minerals. Foods cannot burn. Even if you forget to turn off the unit at the end of the proper cooking time, even if all the water boils away, foods cannot burn!

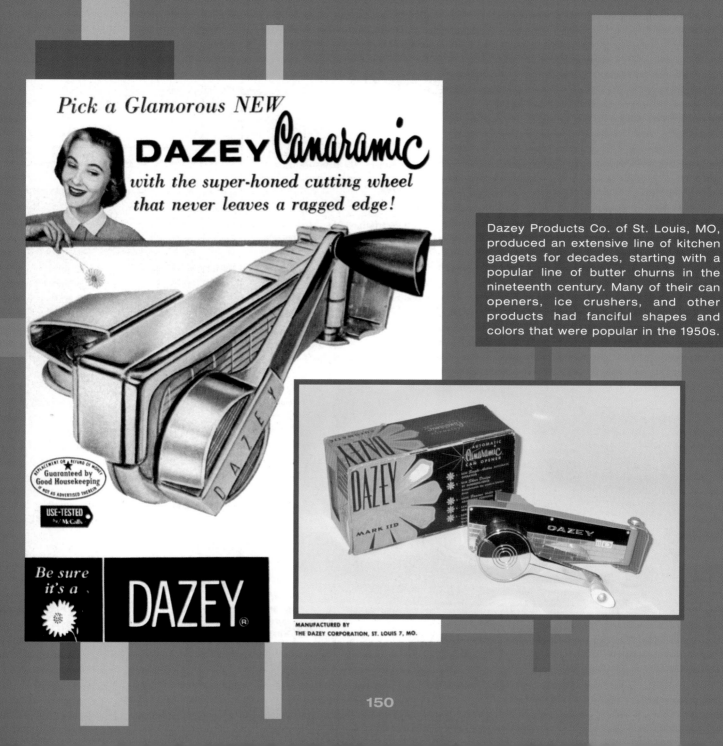

Pick a Glamorous NEW

DAZEY *Canaramic*

with the super-honed cutting wheel
that never leaves a ragged edge!

Dazey Products Co. of St. Louis, MO, produced an extensive line of kitchen gadgets for decades, starting with a popular line of butter churns in the nineteenth century. Many of their can openers, ice crushers, and other products had fanciful shapes and colors that were popular in the 1950s.

Guaranteed by
Good Housekeeping

USE-TESTED
by McCall's

Be sure
it's a

DAZEY®

AUTOMATIC
Canaramic
CAN OPENER

DAZEY
MARK IID

MANUFACTURED BY
THE DAZEY CORPORATION, ST. LOUIS 7, MO.

KNIFE HOLDER
$1⁰⁰

fashionize
your kitchen
in just **3** minutes
with

FEDERAL
Hostessware

NEW! Just Stick It On!
NO SCREWS—NO TOOLS

Here's how it works in 4 EASY Steps:

1 Puncture end of capsule supplied with pin. Squeeze fluid thoroughly over one side of mounting pad.

2 When pad becomes sticky, press against back of mounted surface. Hold firm for 1 minute.

3 Squeeze fluid on back of pad now mounted on holder. Allow to become sticky same as before.

4 Place in position desired. Hold firmly for 1 minute. Allow to dry 24 hours before using.

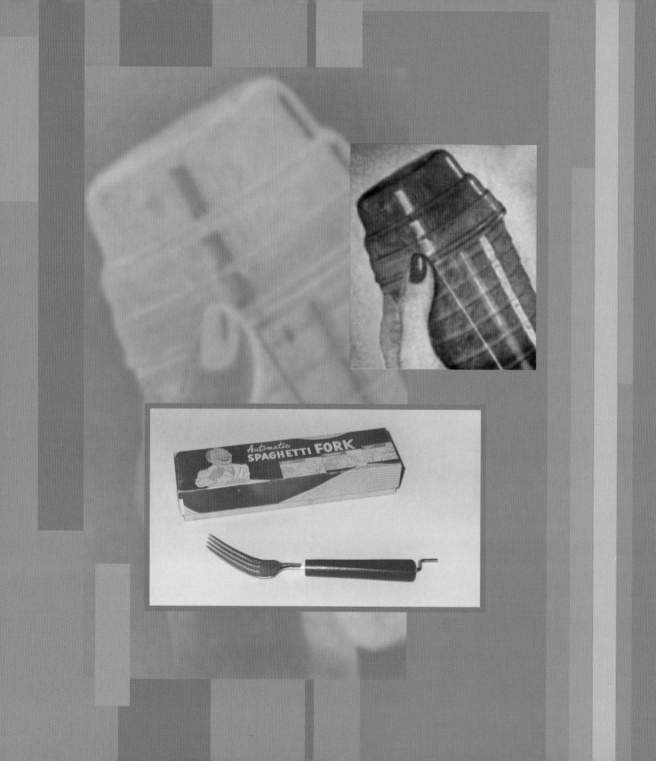

The Jiffy Cube ice cube tray brilliantly utilized the inherent flexibility of polyethylene to aid in removing cubes. This multiple compartment tray also allowed users to form and use cubes individually, which eventually became the standard.

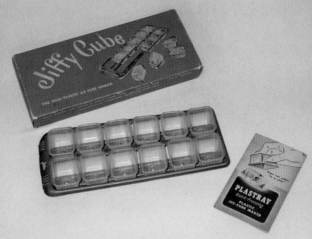

"Gift them with a Gadget" — the packaging of Ekco Products Co.'s 1960s pastry crimper boasted a detachable card that allowed it to be given as a gift.

The French Waffler turned a standard toaster into a pseudo waffle maker. Though the idea appeared promising, it was a challenge to keep the batter from running and creating a sticky mess.

The Kwik-Whip all-purpose mixer was a specialty item marketed as an aid for cooking and for mixing bar drinks. The advantage of this and other similar mixers was sometimes offset by the time required to clean the unit after use.

MATCHING ACCESSORIES
set a Fashion note that makes *Lustro-Ware* a sales leader
T M REG

Lustro-Ware

The beauty, style and utility of *Lustro-Ware* matched plastic housewares boost the morale of housewives . . . make kitchens look their best . . . lightens work, too! *Regular advertising in leading women's service magazines keeps them shopping for new and additional Lustro-Ware items.* They prefer its Good Housekeeping guaranteed quality, love its budget value! It's easy to get your share of this steady high volume by making Lustro-Ware the main attraction of your plastic housewares counter. For additional "sales magic," dress up windows and the housewares section with *Lustro-Ware* banners. These and other free merchandising aids are yours for the asking. Remember *Lustro-Ware* is always in season. Perfect as gifts for the bride and party prizes. COLUMBUS PLASTIC PRODUCTS, INC., Columbus, Ohio

Lustro-Ware
PLASTIC HOUSEWARES
"America's Foremost Line"

REPLACEMENT OR A REFUND OF MONEY
Guaranteed by
Good Housekeeping
IF NOT AS ADVERTISED THEREIN

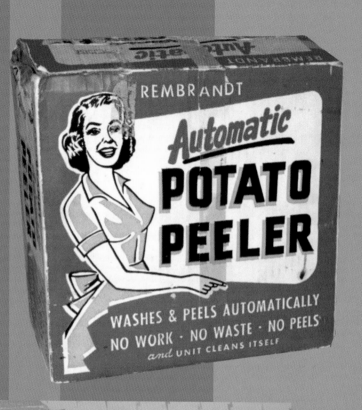

REMBRANDT
Automatic
POTATO PEELER

WASHES & PEELS AUTOMATICALLY
NO WORK · NO WASTE · NO PEELS
and UNIT CLEANS ITSELF

Slice and cut foods with the simple turn of a dial! The Dial-O-Matic Food Cutter from Popeil safely cut foods at varying widths and easily adjusted to different dial settings.

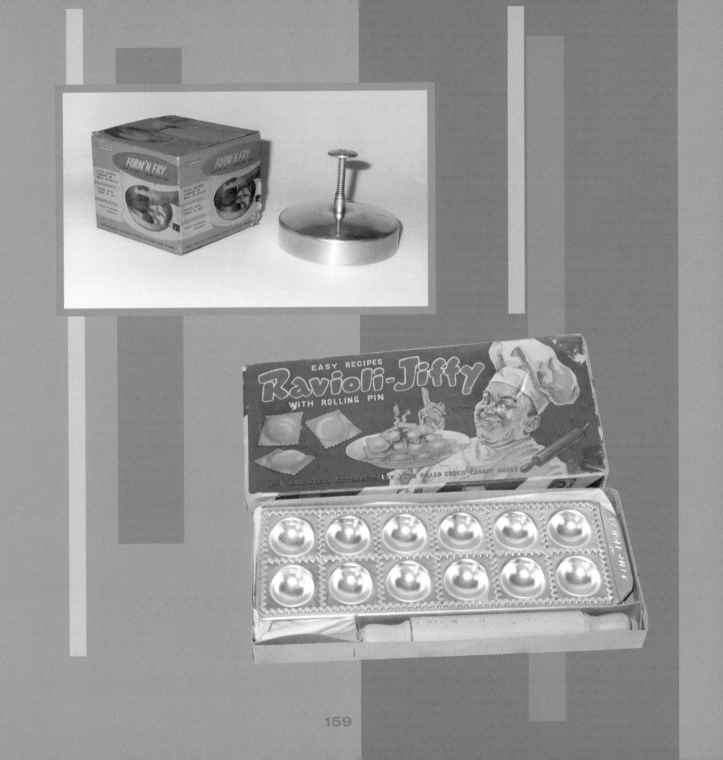

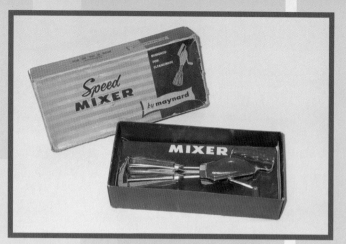

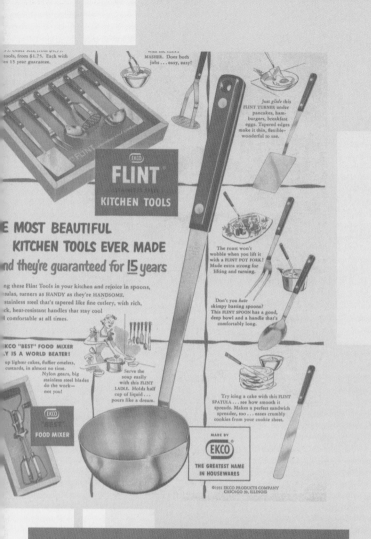

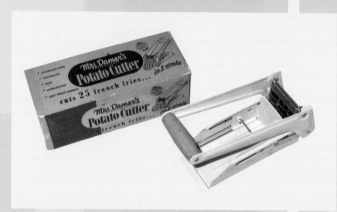

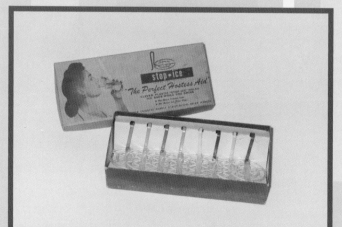

Ekco Products Co. introduced Flint 1900 stainless steel kitchen tools in 1946, emphasizing the tools' elegant, no-nonsense style. They were more expensive than other kitchen tools, but consumers appreciated the added quality.

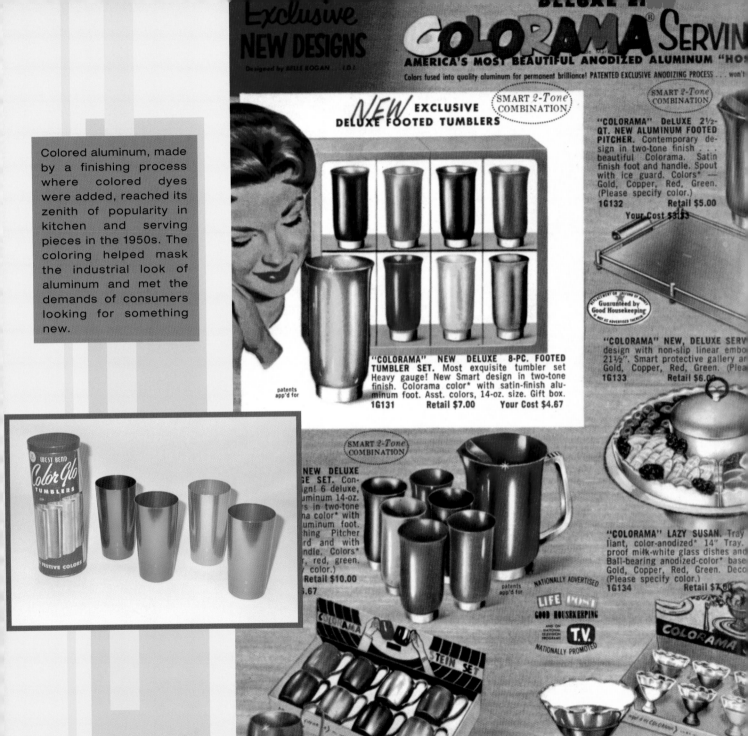

Colored aluminum, made by a finishing process where colored dyes were added, reached its zenith of popularity in kitchen and serving pieces in the 1950s. The coloring helped mask the industrial look of aluminum and met the demands of consumers looking for something new.

Exclusive NEW DESIGNS
Designed by BELLE KOGAN ... I.D.I.

DELUXE
COLORAMA® SERVIN
AMERICA'S MOST BEAUTIFUL ANODIZED ALUMINUM "HO
Colors fused into quality aluminum for permanent brilliance! PATENTED EXCLUSIVE ANODIZING PROCESS ... won't

NEW EXCLUSIVE
DELUXE FOOTED TUMBLERS

SMART 2-Tone COMBINATION

SMART 2-Tone COMBINATION

"COLORAMA" DeLUXE 2½-QT. NEW ALUMINUM FOOTED PITCHER. Contemporary design in two-tone finish . . . beautiful Colorama. Satin finish foot and handle. Spout with ice guard. Colors* — Gold, Copper, Red, Green. (Please specify color.)
1G132   Retail $5.00
Your Cost $3.33

Replacement or refund of money
Guaranteed by
Good Housekeeping
IF NOT AS ADVERTISED THEREIN

"COLORAMA" NEW, DELUXE SERV
design with non-slip linear embo
21½". Smart protective gallery ar
Gold, Copper, Red, Green. (Plea
1G133   Retail $6.00

"COLORAMA" NEW DELUXE 8-PC. FOOTED TUMBLER SET. Most exquisite tumbler set Heavy gauge! New Smart design in two-tone finish. Colorama color* with satin-finish aluminum foot. Asst. colors, 14-oz. size. Gift box.
1G131   Retail $7.00   Your Cost $4.67

patents app'd for

SMART 2-Tone COMBINATION

NEW DELUXE
GE SET. Con-
gn! 6 deluxe,
uminum 14-oz.
rs in two-tone
a color* with
uminum foot.
hing Pitcher
rd and with
ndle. Colors*
r, red, green.
color.)
Retail $10.00
.67

"COLORAMA" LAZY SUSAN. Tray
liant, color-anodized* 14" Tray.
proof milk-white glass dishes and
Ball-bearing anodized-color* base
Gold, Copper, Red, Green. Deco
(Please specify color.)
1G134   Retail $7.50

patents app'd for

NATIONALLY ADVERTISED
LIFE POST
GOOD HOUSEKEEPING
AND ON NATIONAL TELEVISION PROGRAMS
T.V.
NATIONALLY PROMOTED

COLORAMA

STEIN SET

COLORAMA

WEST BEND
Color Glo
TUMBLERS

FESTIVE COLORS

In *The Feminine Mystique*, author Betty Friedan noted that women were somewhat leery of a future full of labor-saving devices. Some women felt that they might be left with nothing to do if they didn't have housework.

ANDROCK
timesaving
FLOUR SIFTER

Guaranteed by Good Housekeeping

SIFT FLOUR JUST ONCE THROUGH 3 SCREENS

One hand does it! Get fluffier, lighter flour! 4-cup size.

Pantry Patterns $1.89
Chrome sifter $2.79

QUALITY PRODUCTS SINCE

Ransburg specialized in hand-painted, metal kitchen accessories, employing a skilled workforce to apply designs in an assembly line at their Indianapolis, IN, plant. Buyers coordinated their cookie jars, match holders, and salt and pepper shakers, among other items, but lost interest when hand-painted designs proved less durable than other decorating methods.

New Color-Beauty
FOR YOUR KITCHEN!

"Country Kitchen"
Cocoa
$10.00

"Chanticleer"
Forest Green
$7.00

"Kitchen Bouquet"
Black
$5.00
(slightly higher west)

"Pine Cone"
Chartreuse
$7.00

Country Kitchen,
Chanticleer, Pine Cone also available
in French grey, light yellow and coral.

● Old or new—your kitchen will be brighter and handier spiced up with Ransburg's cheerful Kitchen Canisters and matched accessories. Choose your favorites from many lovely decorator colors and gay free-hand painted decorations. You'll find them at leading stores—write for name of one nearest you.

HARPER J. RANSBURG CO., INC.
Barth & Sanders Streets, Indianapolis 7, Indiana
Also available in Canada

RANSBURG
Originals
HAND PAINTED

1. Each piece a free-hand painted original.
2. Matching pieces for complete ensemble.
3. Baked enamel pattern and background colors.
4. Odorless—will not crack or shatter.

"Kitchen Bouquet"

Users of a Standfast shredding unit were relieved of the possibility of a grater slipping on the edge of a bowl and taking part of a finger along with it. It had an attached container and came with several interchangeable grating and slicing elements.

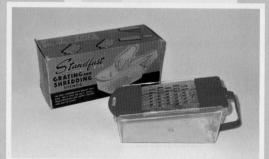

The advertisement reads:

"Standfast" SHREDDING UNIT

The Standfast Shredding Unit is designed to make one of the housewife's messiest and most dangerous kitchen chores easy and safe. The Unit eliminates the risky practice of trying to hold a conventional grater on a slippery dish. It also provides a neat, convenient receptacle for the shredded food— without wastage.

SAFE

EASY TO USE

CONVENIENT

The transparent container and the white opaque cover and handle are made of virgin Polystyrene. This plastic is tasteless, odorless, and will not warp if washed in water as hot as the hands will bear.

The three shredders of tough steel assure a long-lasting cutting edge. They are tin-plated as required for kitchen utensils and—because they are flat—they are easily cleaned and stored.

The Unit is completely sanitary, rinsing easily under the faucet. All the edges are rounded, and there are no crevices in which food can lodge.

Over all dimensions— length 10¼", height 3¼", width 4⅝".

Once a shredder has been inserted, the cover and the container form a solid unit, which can be held firmly in a convenient working position. *Because it "stands fast" it is safe!*

Because it can be used for more than one purpose, the Unit is a daily money saver. When not in use as a shredder it can serve as an effective food-refresher in the refrigerator.

Delivery beginning Sept., 1949

Shipping weight about 16 pounds per carton, containing one dozen Units individually and attractively boxed.

Suggested retail price $1.98

TRADE-MARK — REG. PAT. PEND.

THE STANDFAST PRODUCTS CO.
2146 MURRAY HILL ROAD • CLEVELAND 6, OHIO

Popeil's Chop-O-Matic was one of the first kitchen gadgets to find widespread popularity after repeated showings on TV commercials in 1956. Its pitchman was a young Ron Popeil who had honed his presentation skills for the product by doing in-store demonstrations.

The first cannery in America was established in 1817 in New Orleans, while the first patent for a can opener didn't come until 40 years later, in 1858. Many models and variations followed, with the 1950s featuring some real gadget classics.

Corn serving kits appealed to housewives with their look, matching pieces, and all-inclusive packaging intended for portable, easy use.

The rocket-shaped Dazey Ice Crusher was designed by Jean Reinecke in 1939 and was a welcome kitchen accessory for many years. Outside of being offered in a variety of colors, it also sold with a cocktail shaker attachment.

169

The West Bend Co. produced their popular Penguin Hot & Cold server in chrome and copper models for over a decade. Sometimes mistaken as a 1930s Art Deco object, its main era of popularity was the 1950s.

The Mix-O-Later from Federal Housewares mixed powdered drinks and provided easy storage and serving. After mixing, the beater element was removed to create a lidded pitcher.

CONCLUSION

The ultra-modern atomic kitchens of the 1950s were in harmony with the optimistic outlook of homemakers in a new suburban setting. They represented the ultimate in living, and the colorful kitchens shown in magazines of the era served as an inspiration for many.

Those gleaming kitchens earned rounds of applause as they broke from traditions of the past. The bulky stoves and confined atmosphere of earlier years had given way to efficient, streamlined cabinets and appliances. Living areas in the home started becoming more informal in the 1950s, with the kitchen taking on a friendlier, more homey atmosphere and becoming more hospitable to casual dining and gatherings. Meals wouldn't just appear from behind a closed door; they became a more collaborative effort, with guests participating, if only as observers.

As the kitchen changed as a room, the woman in the kitchen also went through a transformation. Chores done with less time and effort meant more time to participate in family activities. She was finally free to root for a favorite contestant on *The $64,000 Question* just like anyone else.

The Space Age kitchens from decades ago are still likely to seem high-styled and contemporary today. Much of this is due to the slow acceptance of architectural innovation. Visionary Buckminster Fuller once noted that building innovations take about twenty-five years to integrate into the marketplace, but even this amount of time seems insufficient. Many older homes, caught in the era of their construction and hampered by site, layout, or cost considerations, are unlikely candidates for a spacious modern kitchen. Although today's kitchens usually include materials and features not seen in the 1950s, you get a sense that some elements of the past are missing. The lady posing in the sleek gown is now mostly absent, and the more carefree and robust approach to décor now seems somewhat peculiar or extreme.

In the 1950s creative boundaries were expanded using wall-to-wall color, accessories, and spatial drama that appealed to the senses and provided a lift from normal kitchen routines. Preparing meals or cleaning up spills were the same tasks as before, but there was always the sense that they would be more elegant in a glamorous setting. And many housewives were eager to go beyond their day-to-day chores — an adventure not unlike reaching for the frontiers of space.